CW00515797

Richard Maunsell

An Engineering Biography

by
J.E. Chacksfield
FBIS, MRAeS, AFAIAA, C. Eng

THE OAKWOOD PRESS

First Edition 1998
Revised Edition 2010

British Library Cataloguing in Publication Data
A Record for this book is available from the British Library
ISBN 978 0 85361 695 5

Typeset by Oakwood Graphics.
Repro by PKmediaworks, Cranborne, Dorset.
Printed by Cambrian Printers, Aberystwyth, Ceredigion.

The author's first close encounter with a Maunsell 'Schools' class was recorded for the family photo album in the summer of 1943. John Chacksfield stands in front of No. 905 *Tonbridge* at Tonbridge. The locomotive is virtually as built, still with snifting valves, removal of snifting valves commenced in 1946. The headcode is for the Hastings line, for so long the preserve of this class. *Author's Collection*

Published by The Oakwood Press (Usk), P.O. Box 13, Usk, Mon., NP15 1YS.
E-mail: sales@oakwoodpress.co.uk
Website: www.oakwoodpress.co.uk

Contents

'U1' class Mogul No. 1895 poses for the camera *c.* 1935. *J.H.L. Adams*

Foreword

Inchicore Works in Dublin has attracted a succession of talented railway men whose ingenuity ranked amongst the greatest in the annals of railway development. Their influence and consequently that of the Inchicore tradition extended worldwide. Names like Alexander McDonnell, John Aspinall, Henry Ivatt and Richard Maunsell are legendary in railway circles and all served Inchicore Works. The ingenuity of these eminent railwaymen must have stemmed in no small way from the culture of self-sufficiency which existed at Inchicore. Everything which could be made for the railway was designed and constructed there. At its peak under the Great Southern & Western Railway, Inchicore employed over 2,000 and housed about a quarter of the families in railway houses in the immediate vicinity of the Works.

The modern Inchicore is a very different place to Richard Maunsell's Inchicore. It was in the period shortly after the establishment of the Irish State in 1922 that the railway began to experience financial difficulties, mainly due to demands for improved pay and conditions by the staff, but also due to the cost of materials at a time of decreasing revenue and intense competition from road and bus transport. The economic depression of the 1930s meant little or no new investment in the railways while the onset of World War II aggravated the situation. Coras Iompair Eireann (CIE) came into existence in 1945 with the amalgamation of all the railway companies. Dieselisation commenced in the early 1950s and CIE was one of the first railways in Europe to convert fully to diesel operation. However, it was not until well into the 1960s that serious investment occurred in developing the freight and passenger business. Air conditioned coaching stock was first introduced in the 1970s and air-braking replaced vacuum-braking in the 1980s. The 1990s has seen a major up-grading of the motive power fleet with new and more powerful locomotives and new diesel railcars.

At the end of the 1990s a new era is dawning for the railways with the completion of the Channel Tunnel and railway developments in Europe giving high quality, fast and efficient services.

This engineering biography of Richard Maunsell is a fitting tribute to one eminent railway engineer who contributed so much to the development of railways in Ireland and Britain.

John McCarthy
Chief Mechanical Engineer
Inchicore Works 1997

Preamble

Writing about the life and times of an eminent engineer such as Richard Maunsell, who passed away over half a century ago, initially posed some particular problems for the author, as practically all the information gleaned about his personal life emanates from third parties who had little or no contact with him in his personal life, and the task initially appeared to be a very difficult one.

However, there were some areas which could be tapped for clues as to how his mind worked, particularly in connection with his engineering expertise, from contemporary reports, books and articles. For Richard Maunsell, there are a large number of publications covering his locomotives and their performance, but little about the man himself. Having decided that it was high time this latter was remedied, I accordingly set about gathering together all the bibliography in which I could find reference to his capacity as an engineer and manager, which produced the thread of a story, albeit with many gaps. An initial visit to the National Railway Museum library produced some archive material rescued from the house at Ashford where Maunsell ended his days, prior to its disposal by a niece of his late son-in-law, who had inherited the property. This filled some of the oldest early engineering exploits gaps, some of the remaining even earlier educational gaps being plugged by useful data sent from the Royal School, Armagh and Trinity College, Dublin. By the time I had assembled all I could find, it was apparent that a reasonably sized book could be created from all this which would cover much of Maunsell's life and career. And so an idea which germinated many years ago came to fruition and I began putting pen to paper (or rather files on floppy disk via a word processor) for the realisation of an ambition, following retirement from my Aviation career in 1995.

This retirement provided the time and impetus to launch into my task, which is contained herein. I had always preferred to be dealing in research matters when involved in matters aeronautical, so the challenge of going back to the late 1800s to root out the life and background to what became an illustrious career in railway history was taken up. I hope that I have been able to do justice to the Maunsell era and its products in the railway scene, which cover almost five decades of growth in technology as applied to locomotive design, as well as the associated rolling stock.

No. 341, built in 1912 and the sole example of Maunsell's express passenger 4-4-0 design for the Great Southern & Western Railway of Ireland.   *Real Photographs*

Portrait photograph of Richard Maunsell, *c*. 1914-5   *G.M. Rial*

Introduction and Acknowledgements

Although I attended a school which lay by the Redhill-Guildford line of the Southern Region of British Railways, along which passed passenger and goods trains pulled by the ubiquitous Maunsell Moguls, I remained oblivious to the locomotives concerned and, of course, their designer. Trains and their motive power, although of interest in earlier days of locomotive number collecting, were of minor importance when compared to the early stirrings of matters aeronautical which were eventually to encompass my engineering career. The solidly built machines, moved by high pressure steam created by a raging fire fed by a fireman, whom I could sometimes espy energetically feeding from supplies on the tender, seemed an age away from the delicate structure of the contemporary aeroplane. Positively Victorian, I remember thinking. Yet there was something unique about the steam locomotive which stirred one to reflect that here was a virtually indestructible machine forging its way along the track, with a distinctive sound. If one stood close to it at a station, there was almost an impression of life within its steel confines. The majesty of steam seemed complete when it sprang to life at the commencement of the journey.

And so, with these latent thoughts within, I occasionally used to wonder what kind of person could be behind the creation of locomotives, yet never really bothered to delve deep into the mysteries surrounding this classic means of transport. Railways for me were a way of getting from A to B, until in later years I began to get involved in model ones, mainly to keep alive in miniature form what had disappeared from the scene in reality.

The catalyst for this book grew from what became an addiction to railway modelling, with the Southern Railway as the medium. I gradually progressed from early attempts to build my own carriage and wagon stock to the more complex motive power provision, initially by kit-building and finally to scratch-building my own locomotives. The necessary drawings for the chosen types were, in the main, provided from reference books I was accumulating in my secondary hobby of studying railway history. Richard Maunsell, the first Chief Mechanical Engineer of the Southern Railway, was responsible for many of the designs I chose to construct, so it was natural that I should become interested in him as a person. What made him choose this side of engineering? How did he get to where he was on the Southern? Where did he learn his trade? These were just a few of the questions that passed through my mind, as I studied and built scale models of designs attributed to him.

On learning that Maunsell was an Irishman, I was immediately interested, as my wife is of Northern Irish parentage and I had worked in Belfast for some years during my career in Aviation, so had a natural interest in matters concerning the Irish personalities in Engineering as a whole. It thus seemed logical to do some research into Richard Maunsell and his locomotives, and this is the result.

My thanks must go to those who have contributed in any way to the contents herein, in particular Philip Atkins of the National Railway Museum Library for his patient searching out of references during my visits there. The Library of the Institution of Mechanical Engineers also produced much useful information of Maunsell's activities within that organisation and the Institution of Locomotive Engineers. Also Mr G.M. Rial, for lending some historic photographs and the copy of the Centenary menu. He also was responsible for ensuring that the National Railway Museum obtained the personal archives rescued from the house in Ashford where Maunsell spent his retirement days. These archives have produced much invaluable information, particularly for the Indian and Inchicore days. Thanks are also due to H.A.V. Bulleid for anecdotal comments involving H.A. Ivatt at Inchicore, and for passing on some facts regarding his father's take-over from Richard Maunsell in 1937. Also Miss Ann Parkhill for information concerning Robert Coey. The National Library, Dublin, provided much useful data on the historical background of the Maunsell family. Inchicore, through its CME, John McCarthy, was most helpful on details of the Coey locomotives and much historical material. Trinity College, Dublin, dug deep into its archives for me, as did the Royal School, Armagh. Especial thanks are also due to Lieut-Col Henry Dannatt, one of Maunsell's pupils, and Douglas Barnard, a premium apprentice at Ashford, both these serving their time in the 1930s. Their respective contributions enabled some considerable insight into Maunsell's dealings with the training of the new intakes. Both these contacts came via George Carpenter and his long standing Luncheon Club at the Institution of Civil Engineers. Joseph Cliffe also provided the catalyst for news of Maunsell's Inchicore PA, George Hutchinson. And also a particular vote of thanks to Mrs Hayes for permitting me to go through and quote from Maunsell's letters to Edith Pearson during his 2½ year courtship. And, finally, a special thank you to the Maunsell Locomotive Society, which provided access to its voluminous archives of photographs, including some from the early 1930s on carefully preserved glass slides.

All my previous publications have either been of a technical or modelling nature so it was quite a change to sit down and reflect on the 'behind-the-scenes' events which go towards making an eminent engineer. Whilst some of the text is, of necessity, concerned with the technical side of things, I have attempted to blend these with the more personal matters of an eminent career which encompassed the railway scene in those days when that form of transport was vital to the economy of the country in peacetime and an essential logistical service in wartime. Maunsell was not just a great engineer, he was a great Irish engineer, and deserves recording as such.

The bibliographic references are many and various and are to be found following the appendices together with details of Maunsell's designs. Also a list of his locomotives which have been preserved is included, together with their location, so that those interested may go and view the product and, if it happens to be in steam, sample it as a means of transport.

As James Clayton, Maunsell's personal assistant in Southern Railway days wrote: 'As a locomotive engineer he was a man of very definite opinions as affecting locomotive design, and he clearly left his mark on the locomotive stock of the Southern Railway'.

Here, then, is how Richard Maunsell rose to the top of his chosen profession.

Chapter One

The Early Days

The name Maunsell (Maunsel, Mauncel), in which the letter 'u' is superfluous in the pronunciation for the subject of this narrative, can be traced back to early post-Conquest times and is derived from the following sequence of events. The Domesday Book records a manor named 'Maunsel' at North Newton, Somerset, granted to Count Eustace de Boulogne, one of William the Conquerer's kinsmen. The name 'Maunsel' is derived from the Norman French for 'sleave of land'. By the time of Henry II this property had passed into the hands of one William de Erleigh who subsequently granted it to Philip Arbalisterius as a dowry for Philip's marriage to his daughter, Mabel. The grant was subject to two young pigs paid to William every Whitsuntide. The son of this marriage, Philip, married the daughter of Sir Hugh d'Auderville and assumed the name Maunsell.

And so began the 18 generations of the Maunsells who lived at Maunsel House, until 1631. The original house, built by the Maunsells in the 13th century still stands, much modified and enlarged, currently in the possession of the Slade family, who have lived there since 1772.

Some time in the 13th century, around the time the house was being constructed, some of the Maunsells departed for Ireland and a grant of property there. Their subsequent dealings in property in that land are well recorded in the history of Irish civilisation, and it is possible from currently available sources to trace the family back to c. 1290, when one Thomas Maunsel granted Edmund le Botiller lands in Milltown, Clogher and Crossdrummor. So it appears that from the earliest of times, the Maunsell family were important land-owners.

The earliest record of the transfer of assets within the Irish arm of the family under the name Maunsel appears in Irish historical documentation dated 22nd June, 1313, when Matthew Maunsel granted his son Walter the rights to the manor at Lysmerachti. Earlier releases by Matthew of rights and claims of manors can be traced to 1312, October the 12th, to be precise, but these were to other parties.

In 1344, Andrew Fitz-John Mauncel sold some land near Dunleke to Sir John Carew, who was presumably of the Devonshire gentry line. We find Walter Maunsell (note the change in spelling) again, in 1349, dealing with William Fitz Hugh and the Earl of Ormonde in respect of lands in Co. Kilkenny. The Earl also had dealings with one Odo Maunsell between 1328 and 1337.

Matters become scarce from the middle of the 14th century until the beginning of the 17th century, as this was the period of much upheaval and rebellious uprising in Ireland, which in the early days was badly handled by the English authorities.

The Maunsells obviously survived the troubled times, for in 1606, after Mountjoy had broken the Irish resistance and established some semblance of security in that land for the first time in years, a William Maunsell was dealing

Maunsel House, North Newton, Somerset.   *Author*

with the Earl of Ormonde in regard to lands in Garrycloghy, Co.Tipperary. By 1788, the records have a Richard Maunsell and a Nicholas Smith involved with a George Frend in respect of property in Co. Limerick. Richard (it not being clear whether this is the same one as the 1788 episode) is found to own a substantial estate, Oakly Park, in the North Salt, Co. Kildare from documents dated 1826. Also a John Maunsell, is recorded in the same reference as owning Priorstown, Reeves and Newtown in South Salt, also in Co. Kildare. The earlier mentioned Richard was also presumably the one recorded as having substantial holdings in the parishes of St Lawrence and Caherclonish, Co. Limerick in 1847, and later in 1851 holdings in Ashfort and Rootiagh of the same county.

The entries under Maunsell in the main reference work *Manuscript Sources for the History of Irish Civilisation* cover dates well into the 20th century. So a family name that is so well established seems appropriate for one of its most famous members.

And so we come to 1868, the year in which the Suez Canal was a year from completion and opening, David Livingstone was on his last journey to determine the mystery of the streams which flowed towards the Nile and Congo, Grant was elected President of the United States and John Ramsbottom was in charge at the London & North Western Railway Crewe works, with John Aspinall and Henry Alfred Ivatt, whom we shall come across later, commencing as pupils. One other auspicious event took place on the 26th May of this year when Richard Edward Lloyd Maunsell was born at Raheny, Co. Dublin. He was not destined to follow in his predecessor's land-owning or legal footsteps, having, from an early age, 'a craze for engineering'. He was the seventh son of John Maunsell, JP, a prominent solicitor in Dublin who, as we shall see later, had considerable contacts with the Board of the Great Southern and Western Railway (GS&WR), which was to feature in the early days of Richard's career.

R.E.L. Maunsell was to become one of the four Chief Mechanical Engineers to be appointed following the 1923 Grouping of the many British railways that existed following World War I into four conglomerates which lasted until 1948. He was to remain in this position until 1937 and see the railways established in the pattern that lasted until Nationalisation. These early years of the four main railways were, perhaps, the most important in British railway history of the 20th century. The developments that took place during the 1920s and 1930s were instrumental in getting the railways into efficient operational shape for the trying years of World War II. Maunsell, in his capacity of Chief Mechanical Engineer, played an important part in the shaping of the Southern Railway's motive power make-up to carry it through that War, in which that railway was, to all intents and purposes, in the front line.

But before we progress to those years on the Southern we need to go back to Ireland in 1868 . . .

Little can be gleaned regarding Richard's early childhood years at this time, but he would not have been short of company with six elder brothers and four sisters around. He entered the Royal School, Armagh, in January 1882 to complete his education. The time at this old-established Public School was profitably spent preparing for University, in addition to considerable sporting involvements. One record of his sports achievements is to hand, this being the 1885 sports results, in which he won the 440 yards handicap race. His prowess as a cricketer is also stated in the school magazine, in which it is recorded that he won his cap for taking five wickets in six balls in a match against Enniskillen C.C. A lower order left-hand bat, Maunsell excelled in bowling, coming top of the averages in this year, taking 34 wickets for just 109 runs.

He began his academic training at Trinity College, Dublin on 23rd October, 1886, ostensibly to gain a Law degree at the behest of his father, 'to sustain him in a career when he got over his craze for engineering'. Richard had other plans, though, and some brief explanation of the situation at Trinity College may help to clarify matters. Trinity had a long tradition of a pass BA which was the backbone of the University curriculum. All students had to follow this course, with those electing for medicine or engineering only being required to cover it in part. Upon entry, he would have been required to study English Composition, Greek, Latin, Logic and Mathematics in his Freshman years. Later on in the Sophister years it was possible to cut out the languages in favour of Experimental or Natural Sciences. Those wishing to specialise in Engineering, which at that time was about 5 per cent of those students who actually completed their course, studied their professional course concurrently with their somewhat abbreviated arts course.

By 1888, his engineering bent was well and truly established, so Richard was accepted as a pupil of H.A. Ivatt at the Inchicore works of the Great Southern and Western Railway. His father had by now resigned himself to his son's decision to adopt engineering as a career, and had, by his status locally, some

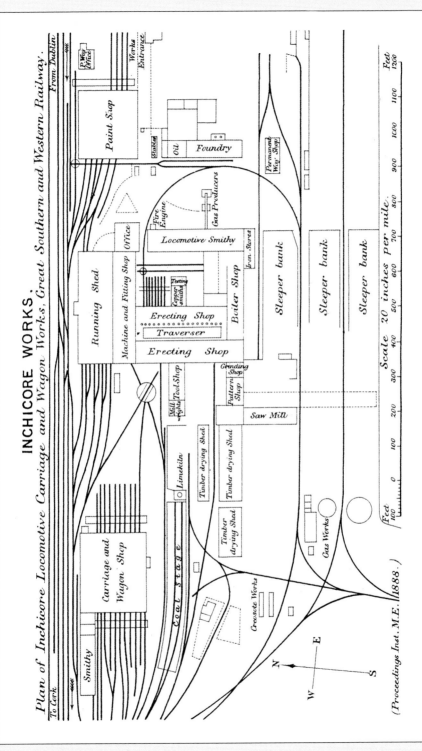

INCHICORE WORKS.

Plan of Inchicore Locomotive Carriage and Wagon Works, Great Southern and Western Railway.

(Proceedings Inst. M.E.,(1888.)

Scale 20 inches per mile.

Inchicore works layout as at 1888, the year Maunsell commenced his pupilage under H.A. Ivatt.
This material has been reproduced from the Proceedings of the Institution of Mechanical Engineers Plate 78, 1888, by permission of the Council of the I.Mech.E.

close connection with the Board of that railway, as we shall see from events a few years hence. Ivatt was heard to remark, later on, that the Maunsell family was 'rather posh'.

So, from 1888 Richard Maunsell covered the engineering side of things at his Inchicore pupilage. Whilst Trinity had a three-year course in which civil engineering would have been the dominant theme, he would have found little of use for his mechanical needs. Minimal training in electrical or mechanical engineering was provided by the University, as such equipment and space as could be supplied for the practical side of these subjects was limited.

The immediate question is, how could the Trinity course and an apprenticeship work together? Students working for the standard pass BA were encouraged to attend lectures at the University, but not compelled to do so, providing that their yearly exams were taken and passed. It is perfectly understandable to accept that Maunsell could embark on an apprenticeship with the GS&WR under Ivatt at Inchicore without materially affecting his Trinity studies which, we have already seen, would not require full-time attendance for the basic arts degree. Obviously the brighter students, such as he, could well adopt this form of study. What Trinity lacked in practical engineering would be more than adequately made up by his tutorage at Inchicore. His cricketing prowess continued in 1890, when he was selected to play for Trinity in that season.

On 1st February, 1891, with a BA degree obtained the previous month from Trinity under his belt, Richard Maunsell left his Apprenticeship at Inchicore and, under the Ivatt-Aspinall agreement, travelled to England for an additional year's experience, under John Aspinall, in the workshops and drawing office at the newly constituted Lancashire and Yorkshire Railway (L&YR) locomotive works at Horwich, near Bolton. This agreement between Ivatt and Aspinall was basically an unwritten rule they had set up, as close friends and working associates, to enable them to offer a wider range of training to each other's promising pupils. The pupils involved had to be exceptional and, in the opinion of either Ivatt or Aspinall, potential high-flyers. Here is the first concrete evidence of realisation that in Richard Maunsell, those in high places were aware of the future potential that was there. But for the perception of two eminent CMEs, his career might not have taken the path it did.

The L&YR works at Horwich had resulted from the statement of John Ramsbottom, who had retired from Crewe in 1871 and recently been appointed a consulting engineer to the L&YR, that the Miles Platting works were no longer suitable for the repairs and construction of locomotives. New premises were needed.

Ramsbottom and Barton Wright, the then CME, assessed a range of sites, but it was a suggestion from the land agent and surveyor to the railway, Elias Dorning, that led to the consideration of an estate to be auctioned at Horwich. This land seemed suitable, was reasonably centrally placed on the network, and Dorning managed to get it for the company at the auction in 1884 for £36,000, a bargain at the time. By 1888 the construction was sufficiently advanced for the commencement of the first batch of new locomotives (Aspinall 2-4-2Ts), and by 1891, when Maunsell arrived, the new works were in full operation.

John Aspinall was the current CME and had taken up that position from his previous Locomotive Superintendency on the GS&WR two years prior to Maunsell's apprenticeship at Inchicore. His earlier pupilage with Ramsbottom at Crewe probably had a large bearing on his selection for the L&Y post, for, as mentioned, Ramsbottom was employed in a consultative capacity, and was shortly to be elected to the Board.

At Horwich with Maunsell, all in pupilage with Aspinall, were three other future CMEs, Henry Fowler, Henry Hoy and George Hughes. All were to be in contact with one another in years to come, in particular Fowler in his LMS days. We shall see the results of this lifetime association in Chapter Eleven in connection with the 'Royal Scot' episode. Hoy and Hughes were both destined to rise to the top in the L&YR, the latter taking over from the former when he moved on to Beyer, Peacock as General Manager.

Maunsell's time with the L&YR in Lancashire was doubly important as it brought about a meeting with his future wife during the social round of events in and around the Aspinall household to which the pupils were automatically invited. In those days the acquisition of social contacts and graces was an important part of the time with the CMEs, few of whose pupils failed to reach high office, such was the excellence of the selection procedure. Richard had also scored an immediate hit with the Aspinall household, who still had many happy memories of their days in Dublin.

After some time in the works, Maunsell then entered the drawing office for further experience on the design side, which totalled 3 months. On 1st January, 1892 his first posting came, as an assistant locomotive foreman in the Blackpool and Fleetwood district. This was not an insubstantial posting, for he was soon promoted to locomotive foreman for the three sheds at Fleetwood, Blackpool, Talbot Road and Blackpool Central which comprised the district. He took rooms at 34, North Albert Street, Fleetwood, handy for the shed at that town, where he had his office, into which he moved the chair which had served him at Trinity College, Inchicore and Horwich. Some 60 locomotives were under his command and he was ultimately responsible to W.O. Mackay, the chief assistant (outdoor), Locomotive Department, with whom he struck an immediate rapport.

The duties on this posting called for considerable time at the sheds in Blackpool, a town not well up in his favour, especially during the holiday season, when the many extra special trains called for every available locomotive being serviceable.

By March 1893, with a year's solid experience behind him, Richard received a strange request from Miss Edith Pearson, the acquaintance of his Horwich days referred to earlier. She wished for a tour of the grain elevator at Fleetwood Docks, which had been erected by the L&YR in 1883. This large edifice, visible for miles around the Fylde countryside, was capable of holding 286,000 tons in 200 storage silos and embodied all the very latest in English and American ideas. Richard had obviously taken to Miss Pearson, and vice versa, for very soon after this a regular correspondence began between them. By 18th April his letters began 'My dear Miss Pearson', but by 5th May this had become 'My dear Edith'. Matters moved fast following several meetings, for by 28th May the letters began 'My darling Old Girl'.

As was common for that time, Richard and Edith (Dick and Edie to each other) corresponded on an almost daily basis, the letters containing more or less a diary of their happenings. Richard often included much of his dealing with situations arising at his sheds, for example the 5th May letter describes an incident at Talbot Road shed on the previous day where a cleaner boy had got rather too keen and attempted to move an engine:

> The first thing that greeted me on arrival at one of my sheds, Talbot Road, was one of the big doors broken into smithereens. I was particularly pleased [sic] when I heard it had been done by a brat of a boy who had attempted to move an engine, which is strictly against rules. I fairly danced an Irish Jig around that youth, but finally let him off with a few words of paternal advice as to his conduct.

As his responsibilities grew, considerable travelling to meetings at Horwich gave Richard the opportunity of visiting Edith's home 'West Bank', Chorley New Road, Bolton. Their friendship deepened and Edith, on more than one occasion, took rooms at Fleetwood to be near her favourite. She was given a tour of the sheds and obviously took a fancy to one of the locomotives, naming it 'Baby'. Richard, in his new-found hobby of photography, kept promising to photograph it, when time and opportunity permitted.

The 22nd May found him returning by train from a meeting at York and being assailed by a lady trying to give him some tracts. Now, he was a regular Church attender, and remained so all his life, but this frontal assault on his religious habits was too much for him to bear:

> I was once coming from York to Manchester and was in a smoking carriage. Just before we started a lady got in and as soon as we started she gave, or tried to give, me some tracts. I politely refused them and then the war began. She raved about religion and in an indirect manner, called me every name she could think of. The first station we stopped at, I got out and then as a parting shot told her that her ideas and mine about what religion really was were widely different and that I was glad of it because if I found to believe her I would turn an arthritic sooner than do it. It wasn't very logical but it made her turn green with rage . . .

Matters ran smoothly at the three sheds under Maunsell's meticulous attention to detail. By all accounts he was very popular with his staff. His handling of emergencies came to the fore at the Poulton derailment on 1st July, 1893, which is described in his letter to Edith on 2nd July.

Fleetwood Station, 2nd July, 1893
1.0 pm

My darling Edie,
    I am sure you will think me a brute for not answering your two jolly long letters, and not thanking, darling old thing, for the two lovely bowls. But yesterday, neither of your letters had arrived at 1.20pm when I had to start for B'pool, and I determined to write you a real good epistle today, and now the fates are against me. - We had an awful accident last night at Poulton, there are 3 men killed and 27 badly injured. I left B'pool at 10.45 pm after a rather long day, and got to Poulton at 11 pm. Just at this time a L&NW train left B'pool and as he had a clear road came along at an awful speed (at about 50 miles an hour) and when he came to the sharp curve at Poulton station the engine left the

road. I was standing at the platform and saw the whole thing. There were only 4 carriages on the train (including the guard's van) and they were all piled up on top of one another. The engine fell right across the Fleetwood lines on its side, and the tender was turned up-side down. The driver was killed on the spot, as were the other two. All the station staff and myself ran at once to get the injured people out and an awful bit of work we had. I wired F'wood for the breakdown van, and as soon as all the people were got clear we started to work, and only finished getting the road clear at 10.30 am this morning. My chief, Mr Mackay, to whom I had wired arrived about that time and after an examination of the place we both came down to F'wood, and he has only just gone away. The first thing I did was to go and tub which I wanted badly, and the next thing was to write to you, darling old thing. I feel as fresh as paint, and have to go to Poulton again to sketch up the place, and write my report which must be in tomorrow.

Recorded in another letter written a couple of days later, Maunsell states his main priority after the accident was to send a man with a pickaxe to puncture the gas tanks on the coaches, to reduce the chances of explosion when any fires were lit to assist in lighting the area to be cleared up.

This sharp curve had, for a long time, been a source of worry in that trains were frequently observed to be taking it at too high a speed. A deviation to eliminate this hazard had actually been authorised in June 1892 and preparatory work was in hand.

There was an inquest following this accident and the London & North Western Railway was accused of culpable negligence in not ensuring that drivers were adequately cautioned about the severe speed restriction necessary and ensuring that they actually obeyed the restriction. The L&YR did have a specified speed restriction of 6 mph for this curve.

Richard Maunsell was heavily involved in the inquest that followed this accident, as was the assistant locomotive foreman from Blackpool, Edward Kenny, who was called to the inquest, for he had actually been speaking to the driver who lost his life, Ridgeway, a short time before the train departed.

Maunsell's involvement in the clearing up of the considerable wreckage and damaged track that resulted from this accident was, according to his own account, completed in record time and earned him some company medals. Prior to this incident he had been elected as a Member of the Institution of Mechanical Engineers, a body he was to be heavily involved with in later years. The proposers for this election were Aspinall and Ivatt, who discussed the promising progress of Maunsell during the Association of Railway Locomotive Engineers meeting held in Killarney that year. It appeared that Richard had certainly made his mark with them and was to be watched and nurtured for future high office.

There was also a further task for Maunsell following the Poulton crash, this being a letter to the L&YR General Manager from 'an old duffer from Lytham' who was scared at the speed of the 7.15 am from Blackpool Central and in view of the Poulton accident should not something be done? Richard accordingly found himself called out to travel on this train and to check the speed in question. Much to his distaste this involved getting up at 5.00 am and travelling to Blackpool on a special light engine from Fleetwood. Needless to say he was none too pleased, particularly as the speed was measured at no more than 15 mph over the stretch of track involved!

Chapter Two

The Indian Experience

The relationship with Edie continued unabated, with Richard taking every opportunity to be with her and, with the catalyst planted following Kathleen Maunsell's engagement to Dr Ballance in London, it was only a matter of time before the inevitable question was proffered, on the 1st August, just five months from the first of the regular letters. Kathleen was Richard's favourite sister, they were to all intents very close, being separated by only one year.

According to the custom of the time Maunsell wrote to Edith's father to ask his permission for the engagement to be allowed. Mr Pearson replied:

Dear Mr Mansell [sic],
　We were somewhat prepared for your letter received yesterday and I am pleased that you have taken the straightforward course of writing me on the subject.
　The objection to allowing our daughter to be engaged to you at present, as you evidently surmise, is the fact of your being in no position to marry and as the future is somewhat uncertain we feel unwilling there should be any engagement. This is especially advisable as I am not able to provide any substantial assistance. [Mr Pearson's mill had recently been badly damaged in a fire and his finances may well have been stretched by the cost of rebuilding.]
　I may say I do not feel much doubt of your ultimate success in the profession you have chosen, but in a matter of this kind, so much happiness depends on freedom from pecuniary worries, that, in the interests of both, it is our opinion that until some more tangible source of income than you are embodied in expectation are visible, it would not be advisable to let the understanding between Edie and you become more definite.
　Meantime I propose to write to your father on the subject and shall be glad if you will send me his address.

Shortly after this Edith was dispatched to Paris to stay with Mme la Countesse D'Anjou at 16 Rue Pajou, Passy. Richard's letters continued unabated to this new address, whilst he reviewed the promotion prospects on the L&YR, taking John Aspinall into his confidence regarding his relationship with Edith.

Work at the sheds continued, and once the holiday season had ended and matters were more relaxed, Richard started scouring the technical press for railway appointments likely to offer speedy promotion to higher salary levels. In December 1893, he noticed the advertisement placed by the East India Railway for an Aassistant District Locomotive Superintendent. Basically, this job was more or less what he had now been doing for almost two years at Fleetwood, he was within a few weeks of the required minimum age of 26 and the prospect of quick promotion was offered. He accordingly went to see Aspinall to ask whether an application might be possible, reporting the outcome to Edith:

I had a long talk with Mr Aspinall about it and he said that every line was so well stocked with its own men now, the Directors seldom picked a man from another line to fill an important position and your only chance of promotion on your own railway depends on some of your friends dying or resigning. He advised me strongly to have a try for this appointment but then he said it was an off-chance my getting it. He gave me a very good testimonial, a special one.

And so, on 20th January, 1894, Maunsell presented himself in London for an interview, carried out by a Mr Rendel, Consulting Engineer to the East India Railway (EIR). By all accounts it was 'a terrible interview', but he was short-listed, largely on account of Aspinall's testimonial. Two days later, he was recalled to London for a medical interview, followed by a meeting with the Chairman of the EIR. As before he stayed at the Royal Surrey Hotel, and returned to Fleetwood to find the letter offering him the job awaiting him.

This was quite a jump up the ladder for Richard, the EIR was the second largest railway in that country, with the important main line between Calcutta and Delhi as its main route. The eventual salary promised of Rs480 per month (approximately £323 per annum) was not quite up to the level required to achieve his ultimate goal of engagement, but was a big advance on that of the L&YR which was considerably less than £200.

The position obtained was based initially at Jamalpur, commencing on 4th April. The Indian railways were, and still are to this day, very extensive. Some 36,000 miles of track were in existence, of three differing gauges, the broad (5 ft 6 in.), metre and narrow (largely 2 ft). Built and, initially, run by the British, they provided extensive communication links for passengers and freight throughout the Indian sub-continent, in addition to providing an effective means of transporting the military around that still sometimes volatile land. Jamalpur is to be found on what was subsequently known as the loop line serving Baghalpur on the south bank of the Ganges river.

And so, after clearing up at Fleetwood and working out his notice, Maunsell wrote again to Edith from No. 34, North Albert Street: 'I was determined to give it a trial - there's nothing to be got in England for a man in *any* profession nowadays unless you choose to wait until you are about 40 years of age. But in railway work it is almost impossible to get anything really worth having until you reach that age or thereabouts'.

He was succeeded at Fleetwood by his foreman fitter, a man called Porter, who was considerably older and with many years service to his credit '. . . a very sharp fellow. But I'm afraid he won't like the running about at Blackpool in the summer'. Apparently, the Directors had wished this appointment to go to one of the current pupils, but those then at Horwich were not considered equal to the job according to both Mackay and Aspinall. This amplifies the importance of this posting as good training ground for high flyers. The next such person to hold it was none other than Nigel Gresley, in 1900.

The previous Friday, he had been summoned to Horwich for a farewell dinner, at which the heads of the various departments were present, Gas, Water, Electricity etc. The function was held at the Chester Arms Hotel, Blackrod and to all accounts was well organised. There were some 15 staff present with George Banks, shortly to become Assistant Carriage and Wagon

Superintendent, in the chair. The dinner was rounded off with the usual toasts, with one to which Maunsell had to reply ('a thing I love doing!'), followed by songs until 11.30 pm. He spent the night at the Banks' home, it being too late to get a connection through to Fleetwood.

On 9th February, Richard finished at Fleetwood and prepared to travel to his parents' home in Raheny for a family send-off to India. His sister Kathleen accompanied him, returning from a visit to her fiancee in London. They boarded the *Duke of Clarence*, one of the latest in the L&YR fleet, at Fleetwood for the crossing to Belfast, from where they would travel by train to Dublin. It was a rough crossing that night, with not much sleep for Richard, as the man in the next cabin was violently ill all night and 'between each spasm he moaned horribly and muttered "Pater Nosters" and "Hail Mary's" in a semi-whisper'. As was his custom, Richard responded to these with 'God save the Queen'.

The time at Raheny was spent gathering up a suitable wardrobe for the tropical conditions to be experienced in India and visiting old acquaintances. His brother Jack, an army officer, had arranged leave to see him off and one night the two of them went to dinner with the Revd Haynes, vicar of St James church, which the family attended: 'He has looked after my spiritual welfare since I was about three'. On 19th February, Richard paid a visit to Inchicore works to say goodbye to his old colleagues there, and made a special visit to Ivatt, who was off colour and at home that day. 'So I found him at home and sat for nearly two hours with him, telling him yarns and listening to his. He is an awfully decent old boy. I'm sure you would like him if you knew him', he wrote to Edith that day.

Annie, his step-mother, of whom he was very fond, supervised the collection of the wardrobe for India and its preparation for shipping. She also gave him a gold signet ring with the family crest and motto engraved on it. And so, on 27th February, he departed for Fleetwood, to wind up his affairs there and arrange his personal possessions for transport. The afternoon found him at the Pearsons in Bolton before returning to Fleetwood for a dinner arranged by his old staff at Threlfalls Hotel. Following the repast, they made a presentation to Richard of a gold watch, chain and pendant. The latter had engraved on one side one of the new engines recently turned out of Horwich and on the other the monogram of the L&YR. One of the senior drivers presented this token of their appreciation to him, to which he responded with 'a kind of shambling speech'. More was to come in the form of a dressing case and cigar case from the chiefs and officials at Horwich, which were a complete surprise to him. After the presentations came a concert by members of the sheds, and to all accounts it was a very jolly evening.

The station master from Talbot Road station also brought Richard a pipe, a present from the head waiter at the Hotel near the station at which he frequently lunched during his visits to the shed there.

The following morning Richard left Fleetwood on the 10.27 am train. Many of his drivers were present, plus several of his officials. As the train pulled out, with Maunsell on the engine, it ran over about 30 fog signals placed on the line by the more exuberant amongst the bystanders, so his departure was well announced locally.

SS *Coromandel*, the P&O vessel on which Maunsell travelled to India in 1894.   *P&O*

East India Railway major routes *c*. 1890-1909.   *Author*

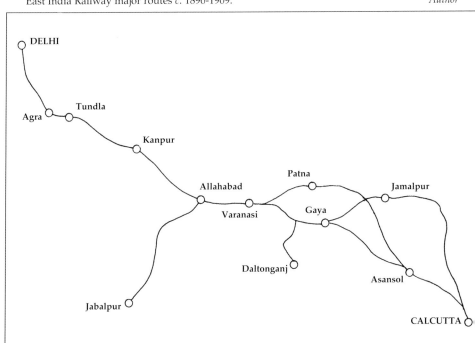

The train journey took him to Bolton where Messrs Mackay, Banks and Wood met him. They all repaired to the Victoria Hotel for lunch before Richard paid a farewell visit to Horwich to say a final goodbye to John Aspinall.

And so, on 2nd March, 1894, he set sail from London on the P&O SS *Coromandel* bound for Calcutta. The voyage took one month, with calls at Gibraltar, Naples, Malta, Port Said, Ismalia, Aden and Colombo, arriving on 3rd April. His account of this voyage makes fascinating reading and gives a marvellous insight into the happenings on board passenger ships in those days.

Within a few days Maunsell was established at Jamalpur, getting to know his new staff and familiarising himself with the needs of the East India Railway, which by all accounts was rather relaxed in some areas. He wrote frequently to Edith, their enforced separation seeming to deepen their resolve to achieve marriage as soon as events and finances permitted.

Matters moved smoothly under Richard's guidance. His organisational skills obviously were recognised by the Board, as on 15th September he was transferred to Tundla (in the same capacity as at Jamalpur). Tundla is a few miles from Agra on the main line from Allahabad to Delhi, and close to the Taj Mahal. Matters at this important shed were taken in hand and after a further eight months the first promotion came, to the position of Principal District Locomotive Superintendent back at Jamalpur. This position came with a substantial house in Jamalpur, sketches of the layout being sent to Edith in one of his many letters home.

By the middle of 1895, Richard was getting restless. Promotion was to be had, but in his own words, this was 'a slow place' and the salaries available, whilst excellent for living in India, were not adequate for his intended father-in-law's requirements as to his daughter's well-being. Possibilities back at home in Dublin passed through his mind, as he stated in a letter to Edith dated 5th October: 'I know Ivatt would give me a billet under him if he had to select a man. He told me so before I left'. In the same letter comes a comment that his father had heard of possible changes on the GS&WR which might produce an opportunity of re-employment there and that 'he was going to run me for it as hard as possible'.

Correspondence from his father led Maunsell to sound out Mr Rendel of the EIR as to the possibility of his resigning should an opportunity back home present itself. As the salary required for marriage was the equivalent of Rs720 per month, it was clear that his present level of Rs480 could not be increased to that amount, and a job elsewhere that commanded the higher amount was necessary. Rendel was obviously sympathetic and indicated that the EIR would not stand in the way of such advancement.

At around the time all this was happening, a further promotion came, this time to the post of District Locomotive Superintendent at Asansol which can be found some 90 miles north-west of Calcutta in West Bengal province. In all his Indian postings he would have gained valuable insight into the needs of servicing and supply of motive power, which would serve him well in later years.

Early in November, a key letter arrived from his father, a letter which was to have an immediate effect on events:

The House at Jamalpur

Top Floor

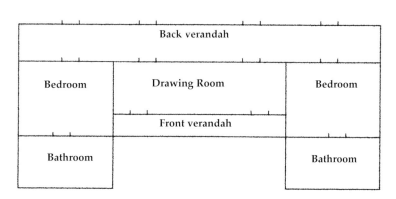

Ground Floor

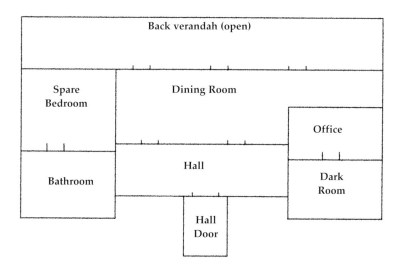

The house that came with the promotion to Jamalpur. Copied from a sketch in one of the letters written to Edith from India.   *Author*

Edenmore,
Raheny,
Co. Dublin.
30 Oct. '95

My Dear Dick,

Just a line to say I received your two letters on Sunday. I called at once on Colvill. He told me that Mr Ivatt had not arranged matters with the Great Northern Rly Coy of England yet.

He has refused to accept the appointment unless he got a salary of £2,500 a year (they pay their present man £3,500). They offered £1,750 which he absolutely refused, and he has now, I understand, written to request a final answer. So I will know shortly what is offered. Colvill thinks it will be off and that Ivatt will remain where he is. It has however done you no harm bringing you before the Directors again for you would certainly have got Mr Coey's place and are fairly in the running if anything turns up. Keep in touch with Mr Ivatt and Mr Aspinall and Mr Bayley. They state you like brides. I will write the moment I hear.

Love from Everybody,
Your Most Affectionate Father,
John Maunsell

Here, then, was the beginning of a series of events which, in a few months were to result in Richard's ambition of marrying Edith to be realised. His father obviously was very well acquainted with the GS&WR Chairman, Colvill, and was keeping in touch with the events on that railway. The Great Northern Railway (GNR) had, at that time, Patrick Stirling in office as Locomotive Superintendent at the relatively advanced age of 76. Stirling showed no sign of retirement and, with no one suitable beneath him as a replacement, the General Manager of the GNR., Sir Henry Oakley, and one of the Directors, R. Wigram, had paid a visit to Dublin on 27th August to see Ivatt, and negotiations commenced. It was news of these negotiations which was eventually transmitted to John Maunsell and lead him to alert Richard in India.

This visit and the ensuing events obviously meant that Oakley and Wigram were impressed with what they found, for at the GNR Board meeting on 1st November it was reported that enquiries of Aspinall and Webb, amongst others, placed Ivatt at the top of the list for selection. A formal notification of the offer of the job was dispatched the following day at the salary of £2,500 requested by Ivatt. This offer was accepted, with the starting date left open, and then, on the 11th November, Stirling died suddenly, and matters began to move fast.

One of the results from these matters was a hand-written note to John Maunsell on GS&WR paper, dated 4th December, 1895:

Dear Maunsell,

You may wire to Dick that if he is of same mind this Board will appoint him within their Loco Works at salary already named to begin with - subject to his reply by wire how soon he can come if he accepts.

East India Railway 4-4-0 express locomotive in service when Maunsell arrived in 1894, one of a batch of 24 built in 1884 by Neilson & Co. with 18 in. by 24 in. cylinders, driving wheels 6 ft 1½ in. diameter.   *By courtesy of the Mitchell Library, Glasgow City Libraries*

East India Railway 'A' class 4-4-0 express locomotive, of a batch of 24 built in 1893 by Neilson & Co. This example would have been almost brand new when Maunsell arrived. Apart from the airy cab, this design is of classic British lineage. Cylinders 18 in. by 26 in., driving wheels 6 ft 7 in.
          By courtesy of the Mitchell Library, Glasgow City Libraries

It is clear from this that a formal offer had been made before this note was sent, for only five days later, and obviously following a favourable cable back from Asansol, the GS&WR sent a confirmation of the terms and conditions of the job of Assistant Locomotive Engineer and Works Manager at a salary of £400 plus free house, to commence on 1st March, 1896. Yet again this went to Richard's father for onward transmission.

We know of Richard's speedy response to this opportunity brought about by his father's efforts, for in his letter to Edith dated 11th December, he wrote:

Now for a bit of news, I got a wire from the Governor on Thursday saying I was offered the Inchicore appointment and to let him know how soon I can go home. Of course I had to make terms with the EIR first and under any circumstances I will not be able to be away until early in February. I have written asking to be allowed to resign but have not received a reply yet. When I do, I will wire home to the Directors of the GS&WR to see if they will keep the appointment open until Feb. If they will, well good. If they won't I shall have to give it up. But I am nearly sure they will. I am most anxious to see how the people here will take my resignation. I am afraid they will be a bit rusty.

A week later he was able to let Edith know that, upon his return to his office that day, he found a letter from the EIR agent saying he could resign his post effective from February. He immediately telegraphed his father telling him that he would be returning early in February and asking him to telegraph back if this was acceptable to the GS&WR Directors.

With the prospect of a good job at the salary needed to achieve his and Edith's ambition of matrimony, Maunsell applied himself to the winding up of his affairs in India, which included finding a good home for his horse 'Budmashe' who for some time now had faithfully pulled his buggy between house and office. His Irish upbringing giving him a good feel for riding, some weekends he would saddle her up and enjoy a canter around the countryside.

That 1895 Christmas was spent in the company of the District Engineer, Highit, and his family.

Maunsell left the employ of the East India Railway on 9th February, 1896, and travelled to Bombay to pick up his passage on the SS *Ganges* to Aden, where he changed to the *Australia* which took him to Brindisi, at which he disembarked to travel overland by rail to the Channel ports and the U.K. He carried with him a glowing testimonial from his previous employers: 'He is an energetic and reliable officer whose services I am very sorry to lose, and I wish him every success in his new appointment'.

It was at the half-yearly shareholders' meeting of the GS&WR on 17th February, 1896 that the Chairman, James Colvill, stated that Ivatt was leaving and that their own Mr Coey would take his place 'assisted by a young gentleman named Maunsell'.

And so, in March 1896, H.A. Ivatt left the GS&WR. for the Great Northern Railway, for the position of Locomotive Superintendent. His place at Inchicore was taken by Robert Coey, and the position of his assistant filled by Richard Maunsell, some six years since he had left for the L&YR.

He was a youthful 28, with several years solid experience behind him and fell into the job at Inchicore with typical resourcefulness and efficiency. His tall figure, with a cropped, military moustache and neat appearance, commanded immediate respect amongst the workforce as he commenced his rounds of inspection on a regular basis. The first rungs on the ladder of success had been negotiated.

Some interesting correspondence received by Maunsell during his time in India survives at the National Railway Museum. The two letters in question emanate from some rather high-born Indians who were writing to see if any possibility existed for their employment as native driver. They make interesting reading, and pose the question; did the sons of Maharajahs also aspire to the engine driver syndrome so prevalent in one's younger days?

The standard 0-6-0 in service on the EIR during the 1880-1900 period. Supplied between 1878 and 1883. Note the similarity between this and the 4-4-0, common features being the smokebox/boiler/firebox assembly and the cab.

By courtesy of the Mitchell Library, Glasgow City Libraries

Chapter Three

Inchicore Days

Immediately following his arrival back in England, Maunsell was reunited with his faithful Edith. With the salary now commanded and a free house, all objections to the engagement were withdrawn. Richard left Edith and her family busily making plans for the forthcoming wedding and, on 8th March, commenced his new job back at Inchicore.

One of the first matters needing his attention was the preparation of the house that was provided with the job. More commonly known as 'Mount Vernon' this property had recently been vacated by Robert Coey following his move to Locomotive Superintendent. Coey showed Richard around the substantial property and the grounds, which he had, as a keen gardener, tastefully laid out with borders and fruit trees. Edith had, by now, decided on the wedding date of 15th June, so some three months were available to accomplish the redecoration and furnishing of the house.

On 11th April, the GS&WR employees put on a reception and dinner at the works for Coey and Maunsell. A copy of the programme and menu survive in private hands together with a copy of the Congratulatory Address to Maunsell and his reply to this. In view of their undoubted historical content these are quoted in Appendix One.

Edith paid several visits to Dublin, and was well received by the Maunsell family. Together she and Richard selected the decoration to be applied to 'Mount Vernon'. She had been living in London for some time now, at 15 Earls Court Gardens, just off the Cromwell Road, and so it was arranged for the Banns to be read at the Maunsell's church, St James, Dublin and her parish church of St Judes, Kensington. The correspondence between them was now back to the almost daily epistle and revolved around the preparations on the house, wedding lists and presents, in addition to the usual descriptions of events encompassing both of them.

With much of Richard's spare time taken up with the house and wedding preparations, Coey had a quiet word with the Company Secretary regarding the forthcoming Directors' tour of the works, a task normally requiring considerable input from the Works Manager. The result was a memorandum to Richard from the Head Office at Kingstown:

2nd May, 1896

Dear Mr Maunsell
 The Directors have decided not to take their tour this month or next. The 2nd July would be the soonest for starting but probably a little later.

Yours Sincerely
Fdk B. Ormsby

This little adjustment to the schedule for Maunsell was much appreciated and shows the considerable foresight of Coey in easing the settling-in period, by removing some disruptive tasks.

Robert Coey, Locomotive Superintendent, GS&WR 1896-1911.   *Miss A. Parkhill*

G. S. W. R. COMPANY'S EMPLOYEES,

Inchicore Works.

RECEPTION
DINNER

TO

MESSRS. R. COEY AND R. MAUNSELL,

Saturday, 11th April, 1896

Chairman	- -	F. B. ORMSBY, Esq.
Vice-Chairman	-	G. D. M. BEARD, Esq.

Pollard, Printinghouse, Dublin. CC.—3508.

Cover of programme for reception for Robert Coey and Richard Maunsell, 11th April, 1896.
Author's Collection

Programme for reception for Robert Coey and Richard Maunsell, 11th April, 1896.
Author's Collection

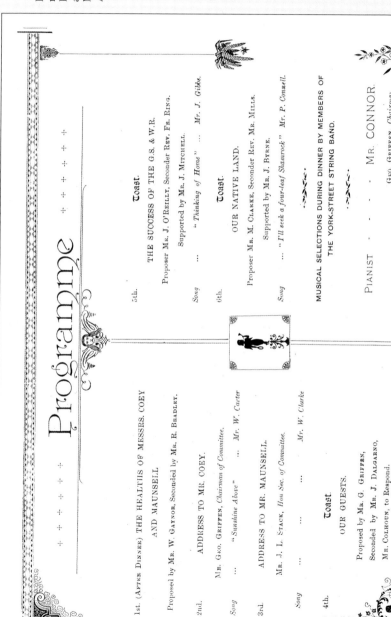

Programme

✛ ✛ ✛ ✛ ✛

1st. (AFTER DINNER) THE HEALTHS OF MESSRS. COEY
AND MAUNSELL.

Proposed by MR. W. GAYNOR, Seconded by MR. R. BRADLEY.

2nd.   ADDRESS TO MR. COEY.

MR. GEO. GRIFFEN, *Chairman of Committee.*

Song   ...   "*Sunshine Above*"   ...   *Mr. W. Carter*

3rd.   ADDRESS TO MR. MAUNSELL.

MR. J. L. STACK, *Hon Sec. of Committee.*

Song   ...   .   *Mr. W. Clarke*

Toast.

4th.   OUR GUESTS.

Proposed by MR. G. GRIFFEN,
Seconded by MR. J. DALGARNO,
MR. COLHOUN, to Respond.

Song   ...   "*Maid of Athens*"   ...   *Mr. J. Clothier*

Toast.

5th.   THE SUCCESS OF THE G.S. & W.R.

Proposer MR. J. O'REILLY, Seconder REV. FR. RING.
Supported by MR. J. MITCHELL.

Song   ...   "*Thinking of Home*"   ...   *Mr. J. Gibbs.*

Toast.

6th.   OUR NATIVE LAND.

Proposer MR. M. CLARKE, Seconder REV. MR. MILLS.
Supported by MR. J. BYRNE.

Song   ...   "*I'll seek a four-leaf Shamrock*"   *Mr. P. Connell.*

MUSICAL SELECTIONS DURING DINNER BY MEMBERS OF
THE YORK-STREET STRING BAND.

PIANIST   -   -   -   MR. CONNOR.

GEO. GRIFFEN, *Chairman.*
WM. GAYNOR, *Vice-Chairman.*
JOS. BYRNE, *Treasurer.*
J. L. STACK, *Hon. Sec.*

And so, on 15th June, 1896, Richard and Edith were married in London, at St Judes Church, with their respective families in attendance. The move of Henry Ivatt to the GNR occasioned by the sudden death of Patrick Stirling and John Maunsell's close connection with the GS&WR had realised their ambition of marriage, carefully nurtured over the years by the frequent correspondence. The situation in the works at Inchicore required some modernisation to improve their productive capacity. The work-force was 1,500, small compared to the railways in England, but perfectly adequate for the needs in Ireland. Maunsell set about with his customary zeal to accomplish the reorganisation and re-equipping needed. His ordered habit of mind was combined with a flair for producing order out of disorder, an ability which was to prove invaluable now and in future times. Inchicore had always had a reputation for quality workmanship, and the changes wrought by Maunsell were to raise the works to the level of an efficient, modern and cost-effective plant, equal to all the demands made upon it as the increasing calls for the addition of modern and powerful locomotives to the motive power fleet became more pressing. Between 1895 and 1902 the GS&WR was busy expanding its area by absorbing other lines, which eventually increased its route mileage by some 70 per cent (this primarily coming from the Waterford, Limerick and Western Railway, then the fourth largest in Ireland). Locomotive and rolling stocks increased considerably and Inchicore became increasingly responsible for the replacement and maintenance of the expanded fleets. From 1896 onwards the works was busy and progress was made as never before. The boiler shop was doubled in size, a pneumatic plant provided and a new powerful hydraulic riveter installed. The machine shop and smithy were both modernised and improved. In his new capacity as Works Manager, Richard had the responsibility for all these improvements, and by all accounts his appointment proved a very wise choice for the complex task.

The locomotive stock before Maunsell returned to Inchicore had been built up under Aspinall and Ivatt, who added to the solid legacy left by McDonnell in the form of a large number of 0-6-0s, the '101' class, and 2-4-0s based on the Ramsbottom 'Newton' class of the LNWR. The 0-6-0 design dated from 1867, reputedly based on the Ramsbottom 'DX' although other authorities have it as a Beyer, Peacock design, and was to remain in production until 1898. One particular member of this classic class lasted some 92 years in service, surely the longest of any locomotive in the British Isles, although little of the original would have remained after the rebuilds during its lifetime. A large number of 2-4-0 and 4-4-0 types were in use for the main express and boat train services, emanating from McDonnell, Aspinall and Ivatt.

Maunsell's immediate chief, Robert Coey, was an Ulsterman, who after acquiring a B.Eng at Queen's College, Belfast in 1876, had started that same year at Inchicore as a draughtsman, rising to chief draughtsman in 1880 and then on to Assistant Locomotive Superintendent and Works Manager in 1886, prior to his stepping into Ivatt's position in 1896, this latter promotion an Inchicore tradition of many years standing. He commenced his time as Locomotive Superintendent with the continuing production of more 0-6-0s to McDonnell's design, plus a further batch of Ivatt 4-4-2T passenger tanks, whilst he and his

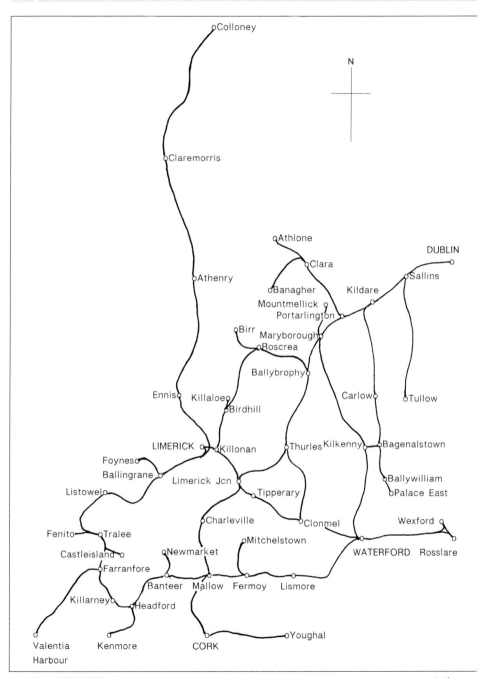

Map of GS&WR as at 1900   *Author*

new assistant discussed future needs in the motive power fleet. New designs revolved around the 4-4-0 express types, which consisted of small batches of the '301', '305', '309' and '321' classes between 1900 and 1907 totalling some 26. These augmented the Aspinall and Ivatt designs which were struggling with the ever-increasing weight of trains now including dining cars, introduced in 1898, and new longer corridor stock. In many respects these new Coey locomotives were similar to those produced earlier, with much commonality of styling. However, there were some design differences as the various classes were developed, the most important being the adoption of larger fireboxes as each batch appeared. Matters in the shops ran smoothly under Maunsell's organisational abilities, and Inchicore consolidated its status of an up-to-date and efficient works by showing its design offices as being capable of keeping up with the latest in technological advances.

In August 1898 the Maunsells, by now firmly established in 'Mount Vernon', received a visit from John Aspinall and his 17½ year-old daughter Edith, who were ending a cycling holiday in Ireland. Edith Aspinall and Edith Maunsell immediately found common ground, the result being that John returned home alone, leaving young Edith to stay with the Maunsells for a few days to reacquaint herself with the pleasures and delights of Dublin. In addition, Edith Maunsell was now pregnant and on 22nd February, 1899, Richard and Edith became parents, with the birth of a daughter, Netta Kathleen, who was to be their only child.

By 1902, progress at Inchicore was such that, at the Board meeting on 21st November, it was proposed that Richard's salary be raised from £400, at which he had started, to £600.

One small incident happened in 1904 which showed that authorities back in England were well aware of Maunsell's abilities. D.E. Marsh, assistant to Ivatt on the GNR, was offered and accepted the post of Locomotive Superintendent of the London, Brighton & South Coast Railway (LB&SCR). The reorganisation within Doncaster works that resulted from Marsh's departure meant that the post of Works Manager became vacant. Ivatt, whose contacts with Inchicore were still active, had, it is thought, proposed that Maunsell be offered this position, but was over-ruled by the Chairman who ordered that this was to be filled by F. Wintour, at that time the District Locomotive Superintendent at Kings Cross. Marsh's job at Brighton was responsible for the appearance of the 'H1' and 'H2' class Atlantics on that line, which were based on the Ivatt design, then the premier express locomotive on the GNR. Ivatt had sent him off with a set of drawings for this locomotive, obviously aware that one of Marsh's first priorities would be to update the express motive power fleet. Marsh was careful to place the responsibility for his first express design for the LB&SCR on Ivatt.

However, the move up the ladder of success for Richard had to wait a few more years, although the GNR episode reinforced the view that he was being watched for future opportunities of advancement, such was his growing reputation within railway circles. Eventually, this advancement was to come from closer at home due to Coey's incapacity brought about by acute stress and migraine attacks.

Coey 4-4-0, class '321' after the first (1918) rebuild with modified running plate, strengthened frames, extended smokebox and Ross pop valves.   *NRM*

Coey 4-4-0, class '333' of 1908 as built with taper boiler. Note the unusual outside frame bogie, fitted to Nos. 337 to 340, in order to cure the tendency for the original inside bearings to overheat.   *NRM*

Had Maunsell obtained this promotion to the GNR, it could have eventually resulted in him working directly under Gresley. How Richard's sometimes explosive temperament would have coped with the strong personality and determination of Nigel Gresley is a matter of conjecture. Most certainly there would have been some friction at times.

The first of the technological advances mentioned earlier appeared after Coey had visited the USA in 1904, in the application of a taper boiler to the 1904-1907 batches of the class '321' 4-4-0s. This boiler was also employed on the smaller-wheeled version, class '333'. The merits of the taper boiler were not lost on Maunsell, even though it was some time before he was to design his own locomotives with this feature (the South Eastern & Chatham Railway (SE&CR) 6-coupled types of 1917), he was always aware of new developments beneficial to engine design and performance. One such development was the advent of superheating, which, until the first decade of the 20th century, had been curtailed by the lack of lubricating oils capable of withstanding extreme high temperatures. 'Dry' steam produced by superheating had better expansive properties and considerable economies in both water and coal consumption were possible. Both Coey and Maunsell were fully aware of this and, in 1908, started experimenting with its application on one of the 4-4-0s, using the Schmidt type initially. Coey was, however, not to see this development into service, as by the time it was ready to enter traffic, he had retired, due to ill-health, at the relatively early age of sixty. His engines lived on, many being rebuilt some 20 or more years later, to be employed on secondary services until almost the end of steam in Ireland.

All this development work on 4-4-0s obviously provided Maunsell with a solid background into the versatility of this classic layout. We shall see how the experience with Coey and his own GS&WR designs helped Maunsell in his SE&CR and Southern days later on. There were also sundry other types to be designed and built, the two most notable being a 4-6-0 and a 2-6-0, both inside-cylindered, and having distinctive Coey features. Both were produced in limited numbers primarily for freight use, the 4-6-0 in two batches of three in 1905 and 1907 and the 2-6-0 in 1909, totalling four in number. It is clear that Maunsell had a large part in the development and production of these locomotives. The exercises would have given him considerable experience in developing what were to become two important wheel arrangements in his future in England.

One little aside, in 1903, concerning the carriage side of Inchicore output, was the requirement to build a state carriage for the GS&WR portion of the tour of Ireland by King Edward VII in late July of that year. The actual carriage constructed was 50 ft in length, was mounted on four-wheel bogies, incorporated gangways at either end and has been described as the finest piece of coaching work produced at Inchicore. It contained a smoking room, reception room and Queen's room, the elaborate decor of these being provided by the Dublin firm of Sibthorpe. This carriage still exists, having lain unused for many years before restoration for official use, and is currently being further restored to its former glory with the intention of being employed by the Irish President and visiting dignitaries.

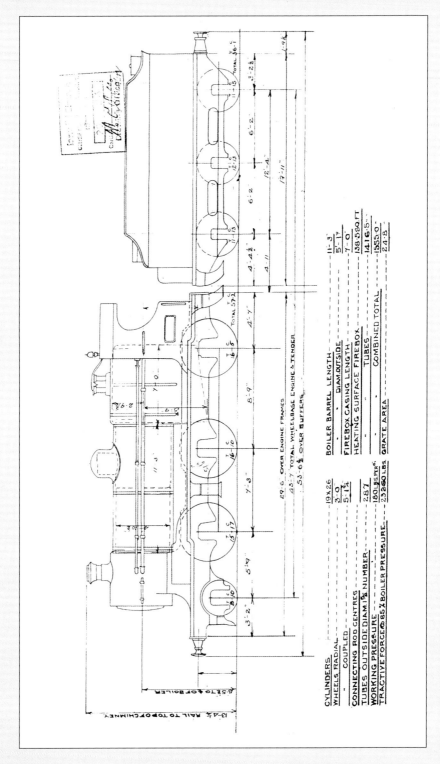

The first true Coey 2-6-0, class '368', as drawn.

Coey 2-6-0, a Mogul by chance, the class '355' as rebuilt from the 0-6-0s of 1903.   *NRM*

Coey 4-6-0, No. 366 substantially as built in 1905, but with extended smokebox. According to contemporary reports they were not very successful engines. Certainly the coal on the tender is hardly conducive to good steaming!   *NRM*

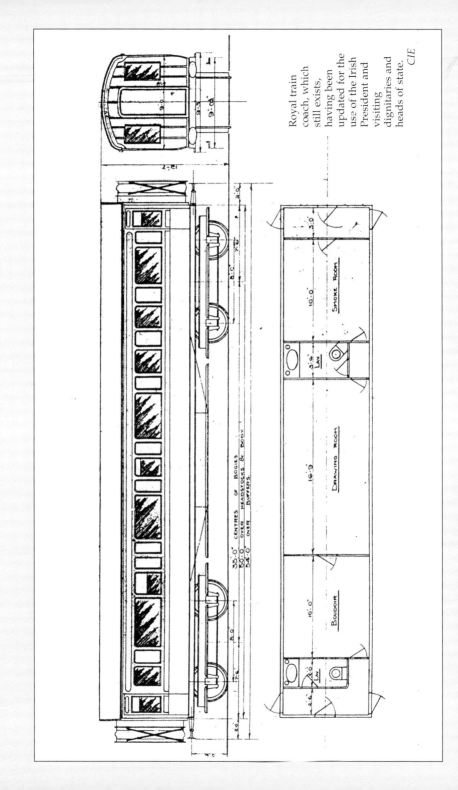

Royal train coach, which still exists, having been updated for the use of the Irish President and visiting dignitaries and heads of state.

CIE

Two views of the restored interior of the preserved Royal train coach on CIE.   *CIE*

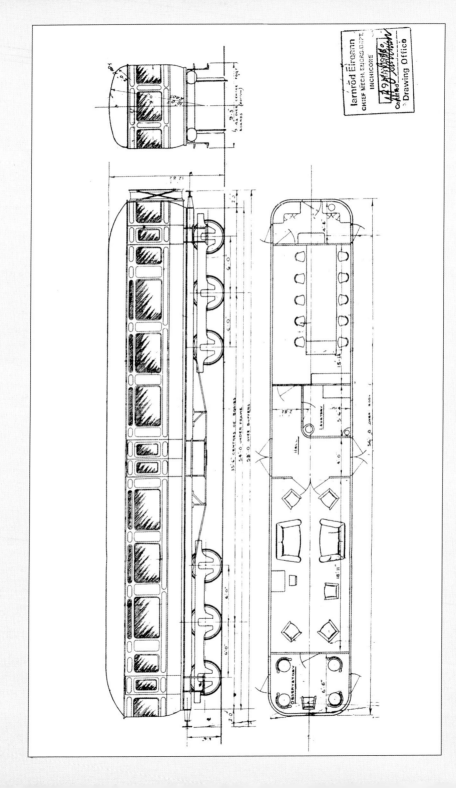

Coach built for GS&WR Royal train of 1903, which actually spent much of its life at Inchicore being finally scrapped in the 1950s.

The close co-operation between Coey and Maunsell, with the latter's efficient running of the works over a period of 15 years, meant that it was a mere formality that Richard was promoted to the now vacant post occasioned by Coey's retirement. The Minutes of the General Board dated 30th June, 1911 record: 'The appointment of Locomotive Superintendent in place of Mr Coey resigned was considered, and it was ordered that Mr R.E.L. Maunsell be appointed . . .' The salary was to be £1,000, together with the usual free house, St John's, Island Bridge. He was permitted three pupils and the notice was the normal six months either way.

Coey, in fact, went on to live until the age of 83, in retirement. He died in Harrogate on 24th August, 1934, leaving his daughter Maud in the family house in Kent Road. Maud lived on until 1993, when she died at the age of 92, but before this she did correspond with the National Railway Museum with some useful details on her father's life subsequent to his retirement. One feature which emerged from this correspondence was that Coey and Maunsell enjoyed a close personal relationship, both at work and home.

Concurrent with the move up to Locomotive Superintendent for Maunsell came the appointment of Edward Augustus Watson to Maunsell's old post. Watson, born in Clones, had commenced his railway work in the United States, with the American Locomotive Co., in the workshops and design offices at Schenectady, followed by a move to the Pennsylvania RR at Altoona. He then returned to the British Isles and obtained a position of inspector at the Swindon works of the GWR, later being promoted to an Assistant Works Manager there. When he was just 30, he returned to Ireland for the Inchicore post, in which he started to plague Maunsell with Great Western ideas, so much so that Richard was heard to remark one day, 'Mr Watson thinks all Swindon geese are swans'.

As a result of his elevation at Inchicore, Richard was elected to membership of the Association of Railway Locomotive Engineers, attending the meeting followed by the customary dinner in late 1911. Two further first attenders at this particular meeting were Nigel Gresley and Vincent Raven, of the GNR and North Eastern Railway respectively.

One particular change in the staffing arrangements made by Richard at the commencement of his term as Locomotive Superintendent at Inchicore was to appoint a personal assistant, who was to be responsible for design matters. The person chosen was George Victor Hutchinson, a native of Galway, who had been an engineering apprentice at Inchicore from 1904 to 1909 and had been employed in the Drawing Office for some time. Hutchinson was to be of great help technically, with his design expertise, and when further work on superheating took place, played a leading role in the development of the type of header used for many years subsequently on the Southern Railway in the Maunsell superheater.

By now, Maunsell had acquired a predilection for the Belpaire firebox, whether by representation from Watson and his GWR background or his own experience on the class '368' Mogul of 1909 (which broke with the Inchicore round-top box tradition), or even his own requirements to adopt progressive ideas is not immediately clear. However, he specified it for his first design for the GS&WR, a superheated 4-4-0 express locomotive. Although widely

No. 341, the only example of a Maunsell express locomotive produced during his tenure as Locomotive Superintendent at Inchicore. *Real Photographs*

credited to Maunsell, this design was, in fact, originally schemed under Coey just before he retired. After some restyling and detail changes a prototype was ordered and built and, with typical Maunsell caution, put into service before the planned production series, in order to iron out any faults or deficiencies. See *Table One* for a complete comparison of the Coey and Maunsell 4-4-0 designs between 1900 and 1912.

Table One

The Inchicore 4-4-0s of Coey and Maunsell

Credited Designer	Coey	Coey	Coey	Coey	Coey	Maunsell
Class	301	305	309	321	333	341
Numbers	301-04	305-08	309-14	321-32	333-39	341
Built	1900	1902	1903	1904-7	1908	1912
Wheel Dia.	6 ft 7 in.	6 ft 7 in.	6 ft 7 in.	6 ft 7 in.	5 ft 7 in.	6 ft 7 in.
Cylinders:						
Diameter	18 in.	18 in.	18 in.	20 in.	20 in.	20 in.
Stroke	26 in.	26 in.	26 in.	26 in.	26 in.	26 in.
Boiler: Pressure (psi)	160	160	160	160	160	175
Tractive Effort (lb.)	14,500	14,500	15,320	17,900	21,100	19,600

The above table shows the considerable increase in tractive effort, for the large-wheeled variants, available from Maunsell's design, largely by employing a higher boiler pressure than Coey. The early Coey designs had smaller fireboxes and, although satisfactory for the train weights of the early 1900s, were proving a little short of steam for the increases in weight still prevalent in the first decade of the century. The vast majority of Coey's 4-4-0s were rebuilt and cascaded to secondary duties in later years. The whys and wherefores of those exercises make an interesting story, but are outside the scope of this text.

No. 341 was fully reported in the October 1913 edition of *The Railway Engineer*, together with a photograph and drawings. Clearly, in this design we can see the beginnings of individual Maunsell design features. The raised running plate shape over the driving wheels employed reappears in the 'D1', 'E1' and 'L1' classes that emanated from the late SE&CR and early Southern days. A Belpaire firebox is employed, Coey having remained resolutely a round-top box man in all his 4-4-0s. The boiler was considerably larger than the earlier Coey designs, with a total heating surface of 1855.7 sq. ft, including the superheater. Piston type valves were fitted from the outset, of no less than 9 inches diameter. Walschaerts' gear was employed, driven from eccentrics on the driving axle. The two 20 inch-diameter cylinders sat comfortably between the 1⅛ inch plate frames. Altogether a rather elegant locomotive, which was claimed to be the most powerful passenger engine on the Irish railways at that time.

The detail design of No. 341 was in the very capable hands of Ernest Joynt, the chief locomotive draughtsman, who worked closely with Hutchinson on the detail changes ordered by Maunsell. Following his education at Methodist College, Belfast, Joynt had commenced as a pupil of Ivatt in 1892, entered the Drawing Office and risen to his present position under Coey. He wrote an

The last Maunsell Inchicore design to go into service on the GS&WR, the class '257' 0-6-0 No. 258 of the first (1913) batch.

interesting series of articles 'Reminiscences of an Irish Locomotive Works' covering his time at Inchicore which were published in the 1932 to 1934 editions of *The Locomotive*. His chief and he obviously got along very well, and we can get a good feel for the industry and popularity Maunsell engendered by reference to Joynt's text: 'Splendidly energetic' [1933 page 275]. 'Mr Maunsell was a very pleasant chief to work under. His energy of character was infectious, and his fertility in new and progressive ideas kept the drawing office always working at full load' [1933 page 342].

This respect was reciprocated by Richard, as we will see in the events which followed his transfer to the SE&CR which involved the 'L' class episode.

Towards the middle of 1913, Maunsell was approached by the South Eastern and Chatham Railway with an offer of the position of Chief Mechanical Engineer, to replace Harry S. Wainwright, the retiring Locomotive, Carriage and Wagon Superintendent. The reasons and conditions leading to Wainwright's retirement are covered in the next chapter. He accepted the offer after some negotiations regarding the conditions and salary, and duly informed the Board of the GS&WR of his intended change. The minutes of the Board meeting of 7th October, 1913 stated:

> It was ordered that Mr Maunsell's resignation of his position as Locomotive Engineer to the Company be accepted with great regret.
> And that Mr Edward A. Watson be appointed Locomotive Engineer at a salary of £800 per annum from 1st December, 1913 with permission to take three pupils.

One further design episode which was under way before Maunsell moved to England was that of a new 0-6-0 goods locomotive, class '257', of which a batch of four was constructed in 1913, followed by a further four in 1914 under Watson. Useful and reliable engines, they were a development of the earlier McDonnell/Coey 0-6-0s, but had one significant difference - they employed superheating from the outset. The initial batch, which appeared just prior to Maunsell's departure had the Schmidt type, whilst the remainder employed the Hutchinson/Maunsell type, now patented so far as the header design was concerned. These final offerings of Maunsell remained in service for many years and two, in fact, lived on until 1965.

Concurrent with the 0-6-0 development, Maunsell had had the Inchicore design team at work on the scheming of an 0-8-2 tank proposed for yard banking work in the Inchicore-Kingsbridge area. This design had three cylinders, the middle one of which was to have a conjugated gear for the centre valve. This valve gear was a technical advance of some considerable importance to Maunsell's later thinking when considering three-cylinder locomotives at Ashford, as we shall see later in Chapter Seven. This tank design got no further than the drawing board, the conjugated gear proving a difficult mechanism owing to the steep inclination of the centre cylinder, and was cancelled by Watson who replaced it with a 4-8-0 tank of his own design. The one significant feature of this exercise was the construction of a wooden mock-up of the cab arrangement, the first recorded employment of this design aid by Maunsell. (The answer to the inclination problem was worked out on the

SE&CR by Harold Holcroft in quite a simple way, by arranging the centre valve in the same plane as the outer ones and imparting a twist to the steam ports of the cylinder, plus moving the centre crank around by an equivalent amount to that produced by the cylinder inclination, in order to give six equally spaced impulses). A drawing of this proposed 0-8-2T shows a definite likeness to the 'Z' class 0-8-0T of Southern days. Richard obviously had an extremely retentive mind where design concepts were concerned and frequently we come across features and layouts emanating from earlier episodes in his life.

One tank which did emerge during Richard's brief sojourn at Inchicore was converted from one of the four class '203' 0-6-4Ts built in 1879 by McDonnell. The iron plate frames were prone to damage when lifting during repairs, and those on No. 204 were deemed irrepairable in 1912. The remedy was to convert to the 0-6-0T layout. The back tank was removed and replaced by a small bunker, whilst the side tanks were replaced by wider and deeper tanks. The end result, finished in 1913, proved to be a very useful addition to the shunting stock and was so useful that it lived on until the late 1940s before scrapping.

Maunsell's one other tank design for the GS&WR was a 4-4-2 type, which employed a standard boiler from the class '351' 0-6-0, 18 in. by 24 in. cylinders and 5 ft 8 in. driving wheels. The tank capacity was 2,000 gallons and 3 tons of coal was provided for. This locomotive was never authorised.

Shortly before Richard left the GS&WR in 1913, there was a strike on the railways in Ireland which spread rapidly until the whole system was in danger of grinding to a complete halt. Some drivers refused to be drawn into this event and kept a skeleton service going. One can gauge the respect in the drivers' circles which was directed towards Maunsell, as one was heard to remark (by Joynt); 'I gave him my word [Mr Maunsell] I'll do my best to keep the mails going, no matter what happens'.

No. 341 was to remain the only example of Maunsell's design leadership for an express locomotive in Ireland for 13 years, as Watson cancelled the production batch and had them replaced by his own design of a four-cylinder 4-6-0, loosely based on the Churchward 'Stars', on his promotion to Locomotive Superintendent. However, the advent of World War I and troubles soon to surface in Ireland in the shape of the 1916 Easter Uprising, meant that his plans to get a sizeable fleet into service quickly were considerably delayed until hostilities were over on both counts. By the time all his plans for these 4-6-0s had been realised, Watson had resigned to move over to Beyer, Peacock as General Manager at Gorton in early 1922. The '400' class, as they were known, were not as successful as their designer hoped, due to their voracious coal and water consumption, and also suffered a frame design problem in the area of the outside cylinder position. They were shortlived in their original guise, being either scrapped or extensively rebuilt by 1930.

No. 341 was withdrawn in 1928, after nearly 16 years of reliable service, it being uneconomic to replace the boiler, but, by then, other Maunsell designs were gracing Irish rails, as we shall see later.

Chapter Four

The Ashford Appointment

The most surprising fact which came to light when researching this book was that Richard Maunsell only designed one passenger locomotive for the GS&WR, in 1912, mentioned in the previous chapter. What therefore persuaded the SE&CR Directors to offer him the post of Chief Mechanical Engineer on a predominantly passenger railway? Maunsell had been trained under H.A. Ivatt at Inchicore, and although Ivatt had retired in 1911 from the GNR, he may well have had some say in recommending the appointment. However, the over-riding reason appears to be the experience Maunsell had obtained whilst in the post of Works Manager at Inchicore, for the Ashford works had been very badly reorganised during the consolidation following the closedown of the old London, Chatham & Dover Railway's Longhedge works, and could no longer cope with the workload required of it.

We also need to look at the stock situation on the SE&CR that existed prior to the enforced retirement of the previous incumbent, Harry Wainwright. The SE&CR constituted the merger of the South Eastern Railway and London,Chatham and Dover Railway, and the combining of these two inevitably led to a large number of small batches of locomotive types of different design lineage, so standardisation was needed, but was hampered due to severe financial constraints imposed, from February 1903, on Wainwright, who was not the best administrator. There is also the fact that Wainwright additionally had the responsibility of carriage and wagon design, construction and maintenance, viz., his official appointment as Locomotive, Carriage and Wagon Superintendent to the Managing Committee.

This latter title implies that the Managing Committee might well have been in a position to impose their ideas in the technical field, and indeed there is evidence that they did in fact try to influence such matters somewhat, but thankfully Wainwright was capable of thwarting their attention with some considerable diplomacy, a matter which must have helped the situation. However, the real trouble appeared to lie in the combining of the locomotive and rolling stock departments of two railways under one person. Was this perhaps an attempt to economise? If so, it eventually backfired when Wainwright's limitations as an administrator of what was an over-sized department were exposed in the statement to the committee in October 1911 by the General Manager, Francis H. Dent 'I think the time has arrived to make some alterations in the organisation of the Locomotive, Carriage and Wagon Department'. Dent went on to recommend the appointment of a new person responsible for engineering matters to the Locomotive Superintendent, over running to the Superintendent of the Line and for disciplinary matters to the General Manager. This new managerial set-up was confirmed in principle by the committee, but was not fully implemented until the appointment of Maunsell in December 1913, by which time Wainwright had been retired at

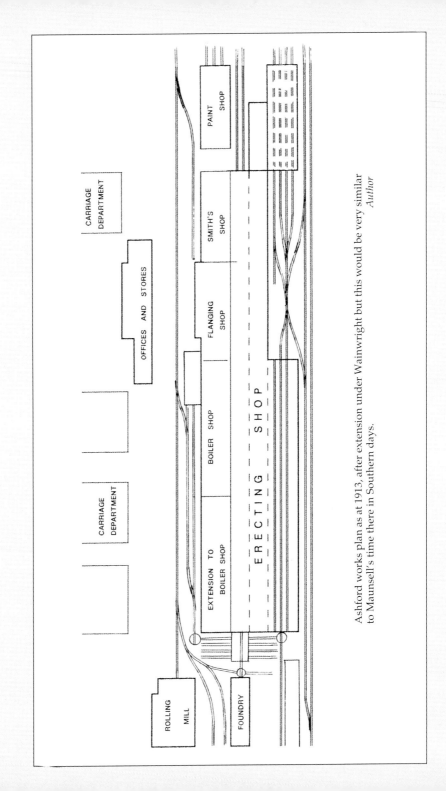

Ashford works plan as at 1913, after extension under Wainwright but this would be very similar to Maunsell's time there in Southern days.

Author

the early age of 49. The SE&CR was in desperate need of an engineering leader to manage the locomotive developments required to alleviate the ever-increasing train loads on this line.

The salary offered to Maunsell was £2,000 per annum, rising to £2,500 after 12 months. This was a considerable increase on Wainwright's final known salary of £1,550, and reflects on the importance of the responsibilities that came with the job. The SE&CR Directors recognised that to get the best, they must be prepared to pay an attractive salary.

What encouraged the Directors of the SE&CR to offer such an increase in order to attract Maunsell? This railway was, we have seen, in a considerably constrained position so far as finance for replacement and new stock was concerned. To analyse the appointment fully we need to consider the Inchicore works situation. At Inchicore, ever since the 1870s, following the installation of the first Siemens furnace, it was expected of the Works Manager to make maximum use of scrap materials - in other words the iron and steel, in the form of sheet, castings and forgings, was to be reclaimed and recycled as old and worn-out stock was broken up. This reduced the capital outlay on new materials, which all had to be imported, to a minimum. Rolling mills, the first in Ireland, driven by an old Bury locomotive, were also installed at the same time as the furnace, and Inchicore became a model of self-sufficiency which was to be a feature of its existence throughout the remainder of its locomotive building days. This environment of economy was therefore present during Richard's time and he obviously became well used to working in such a manner, where re-use of old parts and materials was part of the production cycle. Also Inchicore produced locomotives in relatively small batches, yet always at an economic cost when compared to the larger production runs enjoyed by the larger of the British railways. Building in small numbers at an economic cost calls for good management of resources. Therefore, in Maunsell, the SE&CR would have a Chief Mechanical Engineer fully aware of the methods whereby cost could be strictly controlled to an acceptable level for a railway that only had limited funding for new stock.

Upon taking up office, Maunsell found Wainwright's last design, the 'L' class 4-4-0, on the drawing board. As he obviously had no knowledge of competence of the drawing office staff under Robert Surtees who had completed this design, he accordingly sent a set of drawings to his previous personal assistant, George Hutchinson and chief locomotive draughtsman, Ernest Joynt, at Inchicore, for their comments after making some alterations, particularly to the cab, which was now very reminiscent of that fitted to No. 341.

Today this act of sending out drawings of one's latest design exercise appears incredible, but there are some rather special considerations regarding railways which were relevant at that time, and indeed were to remain so until Nationalisation. Firstly, the divulgence of one's latest design thinking would not compromise one's own production run. Railways, since the 1871-5 incident whereby the LNWR had supplied some 100 locomotives to the L&YR, had a legal agreement between each other that they would not

One of the mainstays for secondary services when Maunsell arrived at Ashford was the 'B1', rebuilt from James Stirling's last design for the SE&CR, the 'B' class 4-4-0. This example, No. 17, sports Maunsell's extended smokebox, which was fitted to many of this class progressively. It is seen here heading a down express near Grove Park in September 1921.   *Real Photographs*

'L' class 4-4-0 No. 760, the first of the Beyer, Peacock batch.   *Real Photographs*

produce to sell to each other. Competition of this sort was unheard of.* Secondly, each railway had its own particular needs as regards locomotive types and the designs ordered were tailored specifically to the operational needs or loading gauges appropriate to each of them, and so would merely be a compromise elsewhere with, probably, limited route availability. Finally, any such detail design concepts likely to be of benefit to other railways would be available via the Association of Railway Locomotive Engineers, at which the CMEs of the major railways met several times a year to discuss each other's current thinking in locomotive development technology. The incorporation of basic concepts arising from this forum permitted the railways to adopt the latest technology for the benefit of all their respective customers.

So, on this basis, it was perfectly in order for Maunsell to send Inchicore the 'L' drawings. However, the recommendations that Hutchinson and Joynt came up with regarding the changing of valve events proved retrograde when they were implimented in the final design. The 'L' class was never a free runner at speed when compared to contemporary types having longer valve travel, which gave a freer exhaust passage. In respect of GS&WR practice they had been correct, but the design office at Inchicore had not yet absorbed the Swindon precepts of long travel valves, and their benefits on free running, so shorter valve events were the current norm. This fact underlines the earlier remark regarding individual railway's needs in locomotive design philosophy.

The 'L' class order was speedily fulfilled by resorting to outside contractors, Beyer, Peacock supplying 12 and Borsig's of Berlin a further 10. Thus the immediate pressure was off Ashford for the supply of new locomotives until Maunsell's reorganisation of the works had taken root. It is worth noting that the Borsig batch, even though it was ordered nearly two months after the Beyer, Peacock batch, was delivered first, literally a few weeks before the onset of War.

Maunsell did not repeat this event of sending drawings away, however, as he built up an experienced team around himself during his first year in office at Ashford.

The job of leading locomotive draughtsman, to become chief locomotive draughtsman on the retirement of Surtees in the summer of 1914, was filled by James Clayton, whose previous employment had been in the capacity of assistant chief draughtsman at the Midland Railway design offices in Derby. George Pearson was persuaded to come from Swindon to the post of Assistant Chief Mechanical Engineer and Works Manager. Also from Swindon came Harold Holcroft, to help in reorganising and modernising the Ashford works, still not at peak efficiency following the situation under Wainwright. Further poaching, if it can be so called, from Swindon produced Lionel Lynes who was

---

* It may be of interest to state the reasons for the 1871-75 incident here. The LNWR and L&YR were, at that time, talking with each other about a possible merger. This merger never took place due to the Parliamentary committees refusing it as being too monopolistic. During the early discussions regarding the proposed merger, it was decided that the LNWR should build locomotives for the L&YR, to promote standardisation. However, after Sacré, of the Yorkshire Engine Co., had organised a meeting of the private locomotive builders to discuss the implications of the LNWR action, a court action resulted in an injunction preventing the LNWR building locomotives for any other railway or user, and by inference, any other railway doing likewise.

'L' class No. 765, is seen on a down train passing Westenhanger.

Real Photographs

entrusted with carriage and wagon design. With this appointment Maunsell split the locomotives from the rolling stock, the combination of which under Wainwright had led to some of the problems precipitating his enforced retirement. One recruit came from Inchicore in the form of C.J. Hicks, who took on the Assistant Works Manager post. This posting was due to the solid support Hicks had given Maunsell during some labour disputes, and it was thought that he may be subject to some victimisation as a result. So, in return for the staunch support, a good job at Ashford was offered and accepted. Such was the measure of reward offered by Maunsell to those who were willing helpers. The strong influence from Swindon in this team was to make itself felt as matters on design of new locomotives progressed, as we shall see in later chapters.

Richard had also offered Hutchinson an attractive job in the design office at Ashford, but was thwarted in this by Watson, who wrote to the Directors of the SE&CR complaining of the poaching of all his best people, and so this transfer never took place.

This proved to be a team that was well capable of providing Richard with all necessary support and advice throughout the years to come. It was as well that these members were chosen and consolidated in a relatively short time for, barely 18 months after his commencing at Ashford, Richard Maunsell was to find the SE&CR stretched to its limit by the onset of World War I.

One small, but significant, outstanding motive power problem which awaited Maunsell's attention was the loan of fifteen 2-4-0 passenger locomotives from the GNR, instigated by Wainwright shortly before retirement. This was immediately settled between Richard and Nigel Gresley and the engines in question transferred. On the freight side of things, a batch of 0-6-0s was borrowed from the Hull and Barnsley Railway. This was not the first time the external supply of locomotives had been required, for in 1899, Wainwright had to fill an urgent need by purchasing five Pickersgill designed 4-4-0s, surplus to requirements, from the Great North of Scotland Railway.

After the initial settling in at Ashford and the 'L' class episode, Maunsell turned his mind to the on-going rebuilding programme commenced under Wainwright. The main classes affected by this programme were the 'F1' 4-4-0, and 'Q1' and 'R1' 0-4-4Ts, all of which were undergoing reboilering: the 'F1s' and 'Q1s' to replace the old Stirling domeless boilers (which were worn out) with more modern domed versions, the 'R1s' to replace the existing boiler with that used on the 'H' class in the interests of standardisation.

The one other exercise involving the completion of Wainwright work was the incredible episode of the two 'lost' class 'H' 0-4-4Ts. This all stemmed from an edict back in 1910, when Wainwright was refused authority by a Management Directive either to send boilers away for repair or to order new ones from outside companies. This order was in force for three years, which is surprising as the boiler shop at Ashford was clearly unable to cope with the extensive reboilering programme under way, plus all the necessary repair work in hand. Matters finally came to a head when two class 'H' boilers went 'missing' having been directed elsewhere due to the excessive delegation practised by Wainwright, which caused upsets and interference in policy matters in the

'H' class 0-4-4T No. 329 on an up local near Shortlands

Locomotive Department by the chief clerk, Hugh McColl. It was this particular fiasco which produced the catalyst for Wainwright's enforced retirement, but it must be said that the Board did apparently recognise that their directive was partly responsible. Thus the severance terms were suitably adjusted for a generous life pension of £1,200 a year.

It was not until 1915 that the missing boilers were located by Maunsell and reunited with the remaining parts as were left following cannibalisation for the repair of other locomotives. With the manufacture of such missing items authorised, the completion of the 'H' class was ensured with the addition of Nos. 16 and 184, bringing the total to 66.

In August 1914, the United Kingdom was plunged into World War I and we now need to consider the War years and their impact on, not only the railway scene, but on Maunsell's career.

The Government immediately created powers to take control of the railways, under the Railway Executive Committee (REC), which had many of its members drawn from the 130 railway companies involved. Although the nominal Chairman was the President of the Board of Trade, he delegated his duties to Herbert Walker, then General Manager of the London & South Western Railway (LSWR). Richard Maunsell was appointed Chief Mechanical Engineer to this body, and so delegated much of his design tasks at Ashford to his new team. This indicates the measure of the man in his selection of what proved to be a first-class group of experienced engineers, who carried on in the absences of their chief with great effect. A by-product of the REC work was the involvement in Railway Operating Division (ROD) matters concerned with necessary repairs and maintenance to that organisation's stock. To this end, Maunsell made several trips to the war zone on behalf of the War Office to liaise with Sir Cecil Paget, the Commanding Officer of the ROD, and his staff. One of the first REC tasks set to Richard was to see to the servicing of Belgian locomotives evacuated to France in the face of the German advance. These engines were becoming increasingly immobilized for the want of spare parts. Ashford was given the task of manufacturing the required parts, which could only be accomplished by reference to the actual examples, as no drawings were available. Much of the design and production staff's efforts at Ashford were tied to this in the early days of the War, which had the effect of delaying such plans as Maunsell had for his new locomotive developments for the SE&CR. However, as the pressure of this early War work was eased, time was found to press ahead with the design and development of the new six-coupled prototypes. This design and development exercise was to lay the foundation of the standard practices used for the remainder of the SE&CR and Southern locomotive designs over the next quarter of a century.

One particular event which took place during the War, concerned an anti-aircraft gun mounting, developed under Admiral Sir Percy Scott. This mounting was designed to permit a 3-inch gun to be towed behind a lorry in order that the anti-aircraft defences might be quickly deployed to where they may be urgently needed. Sir Percy recounts a chance meeting with Maunsell, who when he saw the potential offered by this mounting, immediately arranged for it to be produced in quantity at Ashford.

'N' class No. 820, the most numerous of Maunsell's designs. This locomotive was one of 15 built at Ashford under the SE&CR.   *Real Photographs*

A 'one off'. The 'S' class 0-6-0ST converted from a class 'C' 0-6-0 by Maunsell in 1917, which spent most of its life shunting at Bricklayers Arms.   *L&GRP*

The importance of the REC in the organising of the railway services during the War was amplified in 1915, when Herbert Walker received his Knighthood specifically for such work, followed in 1917 by a KCB. Maunsell himself was elected to the Presidency of the Institution of Locomotive Engineers in 1916, and presided in that capacity at the meeting on 25th March, at which a paper entitled 'The Dendy-Marshall Twin Cylinder System for Locomotives' was presented by F.C. Dendy-Marshall. However, pressure of work due to the wartime situation must have resulted in limited time for him to devote to this office. His real reward came in 1918, with the award of a CBE.

In connection with the ROD work and the CBE, Sir Cecil Paget wrote a personal note to Maunsell in early 1919 which says it all:

> I am delighted to see that they have recognised your work. I don't suppose anyone knows better than I do the very great help you gave us when we started the ROD and all the time it was in the early stages. In fact we could not have got on without you.
>
> We should never have got anything at all through the War Office - in fact it was hopeless to try - of course it is one thing to talk about things as they are now, for instance in our unit which is a going concern, but it was quite another to get it going in the face of the difficulties you had . . .

This commendation speaks volumes about Richard Maunsell's organisational abilities. Anyone who can circumvent or cut through the mountains of red tape emanating from Ministry corridors is a born administrator of the highest calibre. It is not perhaps generally known that he was given the rank of Lieutenant-Colonel in the Engineer and Railway Staff Corps for this episode.

Despite all this war work, and the eventual depletion of his team at Ashford (Holcroft had been drafted to a Royal Engineers' camp in a civilian capacity and was in charge of a Depot at Purfleet which organised the supply of railway material to the ROD in France), Maunsell still found time to oversee the design and production of the two prototype locomotives, the class 'N' mixed traffic 2-6-0 tender type and the class 'K' 2-6-4T express tank. These were in service undergoing trials before the war had finished, and the former was to be developed into several classes to cope with a wide range of mixed traffic duties. The story behind this successful design is contained in Chapter Seven, whilst Chapter Eight covers the tank engine saga.

One small, but significant, exercise into the provision of a shunting locomotive for the Bricklayers Arms depot was also to occupy Maunsell's limited time in the latter years of the War. This need was speedily resolved by modifying a Wainwright class 'C' 0-6-0 to an 0-6-0 saddle tank by the simple expedient of extending the rear frames to enable a bunker and fully enclosed cab to be fitted. The saddle tank held 1,200 gallons. This became the sole example of class 'S'. As with Richard's conversion of the McDonnell 0-6-4T at Inchicore a few years earlier, this locomotive proved so useful it lived on until 1951.

1917 caricature of Richard Maunsell.   *G.M. Rial*

Chapter Five

The Pre-Grouping Days

Richard Maunsell was, it is recorded, a popular figure around the Ashford works, one who took an interest in the welfare of his staff and was always ready to support their educational and recreational interests. He took a lively interest in the education of the works' apprentices and the training of young engineers by the company, a feature of his career which found him a useful member of the Education Committee of the Institution of Mechanical Engineers. One example of his interests in others is borne out by the instigation of the Ashford and District Foreman's Association annual dinner, the first of which was held at the George Hotel, Ashford, in the winter of 1919, and to which he was invited. Richard took the opportunity in his speech at this event to outline the programme of work for the year ahead. The importance attached to this and subsequent speeches at future Association meetings was such that they were reported in the local press, as their content was a measure of the future for the employment levels at Ashford works. With the delicate financial balance of a country recovering and adjusting following an exhausting War, there was always the worry of short-time working round the corner and the effects this might have on the local economy.

Technical advances emanating from the intense industrial activity during the War did not pass Richard by, for in 1919 he ordered that the first electric arc welding plant be installed at Ashford to aid the production process. Also, ever mindful of the sometimes injurious situations which could arise in a heavy engineering works, he saw to it that the works' staff began contributing to a Hospital Fund on a regular basis, his logic demanding that the largest employer in the town should be involved in the development of the New Ashford Hospital. This involvement eventually led to the Southern Railway in later years providing for a complete ward when expansion was needed. Edith Maunsell was invited to open this in 1928, and the ceremonial key associated with this event is to be found at the National Railway Museum.

There is one small, but significant, episode which took place around the end of the War in connection with locomotive development which had an important bearing on Maunsell's design thinking for the years ahead. This was the Holcroft conjugated valve gear proposal for three-cylinder locomotives. Holcroft had, earlier, given a paper on three-cylinder locomotive designs which aroused the interest of Nigel Gresley, who was at that time (1918) considering such types. On 9th January, 1919 Holcroft was invited to meet Gresley at Kings Cross to discuss technical matters arising from this paper. He mentioned this meeting to Maunsell next time he saw him. Richard said nothing at the time, but a week later mentioned in passing to Holcroft, 'By the way, I have seen Gresley and told him I propose to construct some three-cylinder locomotives myself and shall need your assistance here'. It was hinted later, by Clayton, that the actual conversation with Gresley had been somewhat heated! Thus, in February 1919, Holcroft was moved into the Drawing Office and given a free

'D' class 4-4-0 No. 729, on a down train near Chislehurst.   *Real Photographs*

'D1' class 4-4-0 No. 735 rebuilt by Beyer, Peacock (one of 12 dealt with by that company) in 1921.
Real Photographs

hand to develop his conjugated gear, the full story of which is to be found in Chapter Seven.

We need, briefly, to turn now to the events surrounding Maunsell's last exercises for the SE&CR, which took place in the four years between the end of the War and the Grouping of the railway companies in 1923. There was a pressing need to provide more powerful express locomotives for the boat trains now restarted to the Channel ports. The Moguls were only just being produced in small numbers (class 'N') and were being allocated to specific mixed-traffic duties. The expresses were the domain of the 4-4-0s, mainly the Wainwright 'D', 'E' and 'L' classes, and these relatively light types were necessary due to the restrictions on bridge strengths and track loadings current at that time. When it was decided to run these services from Victoria, the SE&CR was immediately limited by even more stringent weight restrictions around there to the 'D' and 'E' classes only. As train loads increased, recourse to double-heading was necessary, itself always an uneconomic way of alleviating matters. Accordingly, Maunsell set about investigating the possibility of rebuilding some of the 'Ds' and 'Es'. These rebuilds were needed urgently, and proved quite extensive. The job of deciding exactly what modifications should be employed was given to Clayton, who was to be promoted from chief locomotive draughtsman to Personal Assistant to Maunsell in 1921.

This specific promotion had come about due to the following events. The 'D' and 'E' rebuilds were, initially, contracted out to Beyer, Peacock due to pressure of work at Ashford in other areas. Clayton had been a Beyer, Peacock apprentice before his Midland and SE&CR days, so Maunsell dispatched him to oversee the work in their factory. Some short time later, Clayton was offered the post of General Manager of a private locomotive works in the North of England. Just which plant this was has never been published, but all the evidence suggests it was Beyer, Peacock, for this company almost always preferred to recruit its managers from the main line railways. On learning of this offer, Maunsell immediately promoted Clayton to personal assistant, and succeeded in retaining his services in his team.

It is just as well that Richard made this move, as Clayton had, during the immediate post-war years, been involved in the discussions within the Association of Railway Locomotive Engineers which revolved around the subject of British Standard designs, for at that time it seemed likely that the railways might be nationalised, and a series of standard designs made economic sense for a national network. Maunsell had been charged with the important task of producing these standard designs, and an assistant of the calibre of Clayton could be delegated to cover this important task. In addition to George Hughes of the L&YR, Fowler of the Midland and Gresley of the GNR, Churchward was one of the leading figures in these discussions, and it was this association with the last-named, and the knowledge that the prototype SE&CR six-coupled types of 1917 were proving very successful locomotives with their Swindon derived ideas suggested by Holcroft and Pearson, that convinced Clayton of the merits of long-lap, long travel valves. The modified 'Ds' and 'Es' were altered from the obsolete slide type to 10 inch piston type with the longer travel during the rebuilds. All these rebuilds were fitted with superheaters as a matter of course. Gone were the

'E' class No. 507.   *Burtt/NRM Collection*

'E1' No. 179, on the down 11.00 am 'Continental' in 1921.   *H.M. Dannatt Collection*

curvaceous Wainwright/Surtees splashers and cabs, which often aroused comments on their elegance. Considerable restyling of running plates and splashers occurred, very reminiscent in many ways of the GS&WR prototype 4-4-0 designed under Maunsell in 1912. Additionally, the boilers of the 'Ds' were rebuilt with Belpaire fireboxes with the smokeboxes and draughting based on that of the 'N' class Mogul. All-in-all, the end result also had a distinctly Midland flavour, as one might expect with Clayton's background.

The 'D' class rebuilds totalled 21 out of the 51 in the class, 12 in 1921 with a further nine following in 1926-7, such was the immediate success of the modifications, the modified engines acquiring the class designation 'D1'.

Eleven of the 'Es' underwent similar modifications, apart from the Belpaire box which they already had, being reclassified as 'E1'. The really only reliable way to differentiate between the classes was by looking at the coupling rods, which for the 'D1' were plain and the 'E1' were fluted. There was a 6 inch increase in coupled wheelbase for the 'E' and 'E1' over the 'D' and 'D1', but this would be difficult to discern without a trained eye.

The 'E1s' were as successful as the 'D1s', proving capable of producing over 1,000 indicated horsepower continuously, and so the schedules of the Continental boat trains were assured and double-heading largely eliminated, with loads up to and exceeding 300 tons, for some time to come.

One feature of this rebuilding exercise indicates the ingenuity and practical engineering Maunsell showed in much of his work, in that the boilers of the 'D1' and 'E1' classes were interchangeable, thus simplifying the spares situation.

One matter revolving around Maunsell's rebuild exercises is, perhaps, worth mentioning, this concerning J.R. Bazin's rebuilding programme on the Coey 4-4-0s on the GS&WR in Ireland. These rebuilds were, in many features, reminiscent of Maunsell's No. 341 in that they employed a parallel boiler with a Belpaire box, modified running plates raised over the coupled wheels and a cab copied from No. 341. This Maunsell legacy becomes more apparent when one compares the rebuilt Coey engines with the 'D1' and 'E1' rebuilds of the Southern. Although Maunsell was long departed from the Inchicore scene, his hand was still at work in the features adopted for the rebuilding exercise, and, as we shall see later, was to be implied in the ultimate Irish design of express locomotive.

There was a follow-up event in the case of Beyer, Peacock and Clayton, in that it is strongly thought that Maunsell hinted on the suitability of Edward Watson, a fellow Irishman, who had succeeded him in the post of Locomotive Superintendent at Inchicore, for the position of General Manager at Beyer, Peacock. Watson was approached and took the offer, but his time in the industrial scene at Beyer, Peacock's was shortlived as he tragically died of cancer in 1922 just two days after his 41st birthday. He was subsequently succeeded by Robert Whitelegg, who was previously the Chief Mechanical Engineer of the Glasgow and South Western Railway, and had been displaced at Grouping when this railway was absorbed into the LMS.

Meanwhile, the design office at Ashford was busily engaged on some project studies for 2-8-0 tanks, both 2- and 3-cylinder variants. In May 1919, the initial studies were completed, but got no further, probably after worries about bridge loads. These designs employed 4 ft 8 in. diameter driving wheels, so were

SOUTHERN
1497

10686.

obviously intended for freight and, possibly, yard shunting use. Some of the schemes for the 3-cylinder version may well have been the catalyst for the early studies which resulted in the class 'Z' 0-8-0T shunting tank of later years. The Ashford drawing register shows that these studies were drawn by William Glynn Hooley, who had joined the SE&CR as a draughtsman in January 1913, aged 25, after training at Beyer, Peacock and Nasmyth Wilson. Having been heavily involved in the design of the 'K' class 2-6-4T and 'N' 2-6-0, he was becoming increasingly involved in project work for Maunsell, and was to be promoted to leading locomotive draughtsman when the team was reorganised at Grouping. We shall come across him again later.

So, as the politicians grappled with their plans to reorganise the British railway system after World War I, the SE&CR, in concert with the other railway companies serving the Nation, was attempting to readjust and reorganise following four traumatic years during which it had been stretched to its limit. Stock was getting worn out, locomotives needed urgent repairs or rebuilding in addition to supplementing with newer types. Much general maintenance of track and ancilliary systems required the immediate attention of the appropriate departments.

The next year was to see the result of a dramatic about-turn from the Government, which initially had favoured Nationalisation, to plumping for the Grouping propounded by Sir Eric Geddes, the then Minister of Transport, which culminated in the Railways Act of 1921. The pulling together of a large number of small companies into the four large groups that this Act specified was to place a heavy burden on those reponsible for the ensuing motive power fleets. And only in the case of the Great Western, whose territory was virtually unchanged, was a newly constituted railway to continue its motive power development unchecked by such matters.

Maunsell acquired early experience in oil firing of locomotives in 1921 when a fuel crisis arose and the railways were looking towards other fuels should coal supplies be disrupted for a considerable time. In May of that year Richard liaised with Henry Fowler at Derby, who was a strong proponent of oil firing, and ordering the conversion of 'H' class tank No. 329 to oil/coal firing using Fowler's system. The coal served two purposes, firstly to keep the firebox temperatures up when the oil was not being burnt and, secondly, to provide a means of ignition to the oil spray. Only the back corners of the firebox were used for the coal burning. Apparently, this conversion was quite successful with No. 329 being used on light local duties around Ashford and Maidstone.

The following month 'L' class No. 772 was fitted with a 'Scarab' oil burning system. This used no coal, but according to contemporary accounts proved unsatisfactory due to the firebox shape, and was removed after one month of trials. Maunsell was summoned by the Board to explain this failure and the attendant expense. By all accounts his usual tact and diplomacy smoothed things over and the affair was allowed to fade into the mists of experience.

Also in June, class 'E1' No. 165 was equipped with yet another type of oil fuel system, this being the Mexican trough burner. This proved quite a success and remained on the engine until March 1922, but long before this time the fuel crisis had passed and coal was the order of the day again.

It was around this time that Maunsell issued the ruling that he should be kept informed of all mechanical failures of locomotives so that consideration could be given as to how to prevent any recurrence. With the fleet recovering from the rigours of wartime use, this was an essential means of ensuring that as few locomotives as possible were stopped for repairs.

Out of the discussions involving these problems, and being ever mindful of the need to search for improvements in locomotive technology, Maunsell and Clayton applied their engineering expertise to matters which appeared to be affecting the maintenance schedules, one of which revolved around lubrication deficiencies. Out of their deliberations came two Patents for better lubricators which appeared to offer improved distribution of oil to the cylinders and axles. These were duly covered by British Patents Nos. 192985 and 202523 for condensation type and double feed lubricators respectively. Both of these were registered in 1922.

The last two weeks of April 1922 found Richard in Rome, attending the Ninth Session of the International Railway Congress in the company of George Ellson, F.A. Brant and the SE&CR general agent in Italy, C. Grillo. This was the last Congress at which so many UK representatives were to be present, as the forthcoming Grouping would reduce their numbers considerably. Maunsell's old L&YR associate, Sir Henry Fowler was representing the Midland Railway in his capacity of CME and gave a paper on oil fuel firing of locomotives. We shall see later, in Chapter Nine, how Fowler's expertise was to influence Maunsell's decisions on the oil firing conversions made during the General Strike in 1926.

Also living in Rome at that time, was Robert Coey, who had by now been retired some 11 years. Although there is no evidence that he and Richard met up, it is quite probable that they would have arranged to get together and reacquaint themselves of all that had happened since their years of working together at Inchicore. Coey's daughter, Maud, testified to the closeness of the Coey and Maunsell families during that time.

Also in the year that preceded Grouping, Maunsell was approached by the company promoting the Kylala blast-pipe design to see if interest could be generated for a trial in service. Holcroft was called in and given the details of the system for his comment. The analysis of the data provided was sufficiently promising for him to recommend a trial, a 'C' class 0-6-0 being chosen as the guinea-pig, and a set of parts were ordered. These parts were delivered in October 1922 and fitted to No. 298 at Ashford in the presence of Kylala himself. Trials were carried out throughout November which showed little or no saving in fuel consumption, although the engine steamed well. Grouping was fast approaching and minor experiments such as this disappeared into the background, with the more important consideration of the combination of the three constituent fleets of locomotives into the new Southern Railway motive power department.

We must now turn to the way in which Richard Maunsell, appointed as CME of the SR, attacked the Southern locomotive needs following the Grouping, his expanded empire now totalling some 15,000 staff. His engineering skills and management expertise were both to serve the reorganised railway scene well in the years that were to come.

Chapter Six

The Transition from SE&CR to Southern

On Grouping, the Southern acquired 2,285 steam locomotives of 115 classes. Such a large number of classes meant little standardisation, a problem inherent with two of the other three groups that formed the four main railways in 1923. On the Eastern section (previously the SE&CR) by far the largest number of any six-coupled tender locomotives were the Wainwright class 'C' 0-6-0s employed primarily for freight haulage, of which there were 109 examples. As regards the other main constituents of the fleet, the SE&CR brought in a large number of 4-4-0s for express passenger work, mainly Wainwright 'D', 'E' and 'L' classes. As has already been mentioned, these 4-4-0s were the result of the limited strength of bridges on the main lines, a problem which was at that time being reviewed. There was also a motley collection of 4-4-0, 2-4-0 tender types and 0-6-0, 0-6-4, and 0-4-4 tanks. The only really up-to-date locomotives were the first 15 Maunsell 2-6-0s and the prototype class 'K' 2-6-4 tank, of which more will be said later.

The LB&SCR locomotive stock embodied a large percentage (69 per cent) of tank engines, ranging from the diminutive 0-6-0T 'Terrier' of Stroudley to the massive 4-6-4T Baltics of L. Billinton, the last examples of the latter built as recently as 1922. The Brighton had a history, since 1909, of using tank locomotives for all types of work, including prestige expresses such as the 'Southern Belle' Pullman service to Brighton. It may have been the success of such use that helped to give Maunsell the idea of using tanks on express services on the Eastern section routes, and the result of this is covered in Chapter Eight. Many of the tender locomotives were of the 0-4-2, 4-4-0 and 0-6-0 arrangements. A small class of 4-4-2 Atlantics and some seventeen 2-6-0s, both designs attributable to Marsh, were the sole relatively modern representation of tender types.

The LSWR stable produced the only 4-6-0s to enter Southern stock at Grouping. These consisted of Drummond's huge express types, in several classes, which included the 'Paddleboxes', and Robert Urie's design of 1914 for a solid dependable 4-6-0 locomotive, his class 'H15', which was a complete departure from Drummond's four-cylinder complex efforts, some of which employed dissimilar valve gear for inside and outside cylinders. The 'H15' was a simple two-cylinder engine with high running plates and external valve gear, was simple to maintain and, eventually, in its three developed versions attributable to Maunsell, was to become the backbone of the Southern's express and heavy mixed-traffic fleet. The Urie 'N15' class was first introduced in 1918 with their 6 ft 7 in. driving wheels, and these were followed by the 'S15s' from 1920 with their 5 ft 7 in. driving wheels making them useful mixed-traffic engines. There were a large number of elderly, but dependable, 4-4-0s, again largely Adams' and Drummond designs plus assorted tanks from the same Victorian lineage, the most archaic being the 2-4-0 well tanks of Beattie dating from 1874.

One of the first decisions to be made by the newly constituted Board was the choice of who was to be appointed to the position of Chief Mechanical Engineer for the Southern. Three possibilities presented themselves; Urie, Maunsell or Billinton. Robert Urie was 69, had had a distinguished career on the LSWR, firstly on the arrangement of the transfer of production facilities from Nine Elms to Eastleigh, where he subsequently was Works Manager, and then becoming Chief Mechanical Engineer after the death of Drummond in 1912. Although originally offered the post, he indicated that the limited time he could give meant that a successor needed to be found quickly, and offered no opposition to retirement, so the selection naturally devolved to Richard Maunsell and Lawson Billinton. The latter was only 39, the son of R.J. Billinton who had been Locomotive Superintendent of the LB&SCR from 1890 to 1905, so one might think that he would have had a good chance. However, he had been away during the War years and was a thoroughly 'Brighton' man in outlook. It has also been suggested that his title of 'Locomotive Superintendent' might have also influenced the Board's decision, although this was merely a quirk of the LB&SCR's particular penchant for titles.   The position of Locomotive Superintendent on that railway was, to all intents and purposes, identical in scope and responsibility to the Chief Mechanical Engineers of other railways.

Maunsell, now 54, had a wealth of experience to offer from his GS&WR and SE&CR posts, the former involving 15 years as a highly capable Works Manager followed by two years as CME, the latter as CME for 10 years, plus having been involved with the Railway Executive Committee during the War. He had a reputation of being an engineer at the fore-front of developments. His integrity was faultless and such of his locomotives as were then in service were proving themselves as sturdy and reliable machines. We have seen that one of Richard Maunsell's most important decisions at Ashford was to consider and then adopt many well-proved and technically advanced Swindon ideas. Taper boilers, top feed, Belpaire fireboxes, long-travel, long lap valves were all adopted on new designs. Some other Swindon features such as low degree superheat and inside valve gear were, however, to be displaced by high degree superheat and outside Walschaerts' gear respectively.   The former offering even better economy and the latter ease of maintenance. This acceptance of the best features proved on the Great Western showed that Richard's grasp of the technical aspects of locomotive design likely to result in economical, reliable engines was well founded and the future development of motive power on the Southern Railway was assured of following the latest technical advances. Additionally, he had, during his time at Ashford, shown himself always ready to consider, and experiment with, radical design features which offered an improvement in performance or economy.   Once the traumatic events surrounding the War were over, and the railways were settling back to normal peacetime schedules, he instigated a comprehensive series of tests on all new or modified designs as they took to the road. It was through these and other attributes that the Board of the Southern weighed up the situation as to the selection of the best person to take the CME position. They recognised an outstanding engineer and manager when they saw one.

Thus, Sir Herbert Walker and the Board of the Southern Railway duly selected Richard Maunsell to be their Chief Mechanical Engineer. Billinton's disappointment was alleviated by a generous 'golden handshake' to bow out of the running, rather than be offered a lower post in the engineering department, with the inevitable friction that would have been caused by mixing Brighton ideas with those set up so successfully at Ashford.

One factor in the design and development of steam locomotives which had obviously helped the Board's decision was the way in which a reasonably acceptable design could, by detail improvements, be turned into an outstanding performer. As we have already seen, Maunsell had done just this by his rebuilding of the Wainwright 'D' and 'E' class 4-4-0s in the last years of the SE&CR. And on a railway which was planning a large investment into the expansion of the electrification of suburban and main lines, investment likely to restrict capital outlay on new locomotives, this relatively inexpensive form of improving the capabilities of older designs was a logical way in which to accomplish the ambitious programme of electrification and, at the same time, ensure that adequate steam motive power was always available to meet anticipated demands. Maunsell, throughout his time with the Southern, was always to be aware of this fact. And when one looks at the complete scene, we find that just four *new* classes of locomotives, the 'Lord Nelson', 'Schools', 'Z' and 'Q', were to appear. Some may say what about the 'W' class? But this class was, as we shall see, a derivative of the Moguls, all four versions of which were based on the 1917 'N' variant.

Maunsell's first priority, upon taking office, was to select his team. On the locomotive side the vast majority of this team, certainly all of those in senior positions, were to be his previous SE&CR associates. George Pearson became Assistant Chief Mechanical Engineer (Locomotives), James Clayton remained Personal Assistant, Harold Holcroft took control of the Drawing Office at Waterloo, C.J. Hicks remained in the works area and with Lionel Lynes, T.S. Finlayson and Surrey Warner all combined to make a very strong team, the core of which was based at Waterloo. Administration and delegation were two of Richard's greatest attributes. He chose his staff with great care and defined their exact duties. No overlapping of tasks was permitted, they all knew their field of operations - rather like a Prime Minister and his ministers in the Cabinet, to paraphrase Holcroft. Regular meetings were held, at which the CME presided, with policy, future trends and new stock provision being discussed. All-in-all, a well organised and tightly run ship. A very effective team it proved to be, to remain virtually unchanged throughout the following 14 years, as they all realised that Maunsell was a good delegator, a first-class administrator on top of being a very capable production engineer, and so engendered the respect of all those under him.

The second problem to be solved was the reorganisation of the works: Ashford, Brighton and Eastleigh. The last-named was the most extensive and up-to-date, and continued to be a major production centre. Brighton, a cramped and fairly small works was intended to be allowed to run down to a maintenance only centre before eventual closure, although later events were to reverse this policy. Ashford continued as a production and maintenance facility. Chapter Nine covers the works situation in greater detail.

The Waterloo offices for the CME and his immediate team were not ideally placed for control of Maunsell's far-flung empire. However, he ensured that he made regular visits to the works, during which he took stock of the relevant situations, firing questions concerning design, manufacture and servicing at his managers. So probing and relevant were his requests that some likened it to 'fielding in the slips when Bradman was batting'. In the setting up and consolidation of the team at Waterloo, Maunsell became known to a wide circle of business associates as a man whose word was indeed his bond. His perception of all railway matters was very keen, and he was speedy in his sizing up of a situation affecting him or his staff. Decisions, again, were made equally speedily, the judgements that ensued always of a high order, and were ones which took account of the others involved. Never known to be unfair to anyone, he had a knack of passing his natural sense of fair play to those who worked for him, which ensured that they reciprocated by the giving of their best. A true leader.

In addition to his new responsibilities at Waterloo, Richard was elected to the Council of the Institution of Mechanical Engineers in February 1923, and just a month later his expertise had him on both the Publications and Library, and General Purposes Committees. His frequent visits to the Institution often brought him into contact with Henry Ivatt, who had been elected to the Vice-Presidency in 1922, a post which Richard himself was to hold in later years. Ivatt was delighted to see his old pupil, now at the top of his profession, and many an Inchicore memory was aired. Sadly, Ivatt's health took a turn for the worse later that year and he died on 23rd October at his home at Haywards Heath, where he had enjoyed 12 years of retirement. Amongst those who mourned his passing were a group of eminent engineers, Maunsell, Aspinall and Gresley to name but a few, who paid their last respects to one who had inspired and guided them in earlier years.

One of the outstanding items on Maunsell's list of tasks at Waterloo was the need to set up a dedicated Locomotive Testing Section for footplate and other testing of locomotives. The SE&CR, before he took over as CME, had no systematic testing of engines' programme, such observation of their performance being obtained via the footplate inspectors in the course of their duties. This had been noted by Maunsell in 1913, but the onset of the War, followed by the lead into Grouping, had diverted his attention to more pressing matters. As an interim measure, during the early days of Grouping, Holcroft had been drafted into independent footplate testing to obtain a better picture of the capabilities and limitations of much of the locomotive stock. (For a complete assessment of these trials Holcroft's book *Locomotive Adventure* covers them in considerable detail in Volume 2, in addition giving a good insight into the probing mind of Maunsell and the way in which he systematically approached the testing.)

Holcroft had earlier impressed Maunsell with his grasp of practical locomotive design matters, largely through his conjugated valve gear invention and development (which is covered in Chapter Seven) and was short-listed in Richard's mind as a replacement for Clayton, who was increasingly beset with the onset of arthritis, so much so that it was at one time thought that early retirement on health grounds might be necessary. The make-up of the Waterloo team was deliberately set with this eventuality in mind. However, such treatment as was then available ensured that Clayton was able to continue in his PA role until Maunsell retired, although with increasing handicaps.

The sheer size of the four railway companies needs to be considered when assessing the scope of responsibilities of the respective Chief Mechanical Engineers. 'The Big Four' as they were colloquially known, met often to weigh up and discuss the current engineering problems that confronted them all, and the figures of Collett, Gresley and Fowler were often to be seen striding purposefully along the corridors at Waterloo as they met with Richard Maunsell in his office, which he had decorated with a SE&CR vice and tool kit as a constant reminder of the importance of quality engineering. Under these four men came the responsibilities associated with the design, production and maintenance of all British railway motive power and rolling stock. The pressures under which they operated were considerable and did, eventually, take their toll; for Maunsell the accentuation of his ill-health in the 1930s and, tragically, death in service for Gresley in 1941. Each of these eminent engineers had his own particular brand of design features for his locomotives and the cross-fertilisation of ideas may, in some instances, have been somewhat restricted by personal fancies, although all were capable of adopting good technical advances when they presented themselves. Maunsell was particularly adept at this, evidenced by his selection of his team in the early days at Ashford, which injected all the beneficial Swindon practices to excellent effect.

As we already mentioned, there was one feature of the Southern which influenced what Maunsell could do from the start of his sojourn as CME. This was the large capital expenditure being allocated to the extensive electrification programme necessarily restricting funds for new locomotive stock. This was alleviated to a small extent by cascading the displaced suburban passenger types to secondary services previously catered for by ageing and obsolescent classes listed for withdrawal and replacement. Standardisation to the degree practised by Stanier and Collett on the LMS and GWR respectively was not possible and so the Southern was to become a paradise for enthusiasts searching for historic locomotives.

To his credit, Maunsell co-operated fully from the outset with Alfred Raworth, the engineer for New Works, on the electrification issue so that the transition from steam to electric passenger services was smooth. Freight services, however, were still to remain very much the province of steam.

We now need to assess Maunsell's first locomotive development for the Southern, which evolved from a requirement to provide more express locomotives capable of dealing with 400 ton trains in all regions.

At the time Maunsell had been settling in on the SE&CR at Ashford before the War, events were moving on the LSWR under its new Chief Mechanical Engineer, Robert Urie, who had taken over following the death in service of Dugald Drummond in 1912. Robert Urie had swept aside Drummond's complex approach to the 4-6-0 as described earlier, with the first example of his locomotives being the 'H15' class of 1913. In many respects the basic design concept of these locomotives was very similar to that of the British Railways standard 4-6-0 of the 1950s. In his design, Urie showed his forward thinking in terms of ease of maintenance by adopting the outside cylinders and valve gear. This was very much in line with Richard Maunsell's new designs then on the drawing board for the SE&CR.

Urie 'H15' class 4-6-0 No. 489 c. 1935.

I.H.L. Adams

A total of 15 'H15s' were built (1913-14), plus 20 'N15s' (1919-23) and 20 'S15s' (1920-21), the major differences between the types being the coupled wheel diameters of 6 ft, 6 ft 7 in. and 5 ft 7 in. respectively. The 'H15' class was also the only marque to have a parallel boiler, not immediately apparent, and could be better identified by the raised running plate over the cylinders. All were superheated when built, save two early examples of the 'H15'. The 'N15s' were primarily for express passenger work, whereas the 'H15s' and 'S15s' were for mixed traffic. The performance of all these classes, although satisfactory enough to cover the train weights then current on the Western Section at Grouping, was hampered by poor steaming qualities. Their reliability, however, was legendary, and the ease of servicing a great bonus due to the ease of accessibility designed in by Urie for the motion. The superheaters were a bit of a problem when maintenance was called for, in that Urie designed them without taking stock of the need to have quick and free access to the boiler tubes. The Eastleigh superheater as then fitted to the large 4-6-0s consisted of two headers connected by a series of vertical headers into which the superheater elements were fitted. This collection of castings presented a considerable resistance to the gas flows and also impeded the cleaning of the boiler tubes. Both these features had a detrimental effect on the efficiency of the boiler and, as the engines so fitted came in for heavy repairs Maunsell ordered that the superheaters be changed for his own version, devised by himself and Hutchinson during his Inchicore days and subsequently adopted at Ashford on all new designs and rebuilds.

Having taken stock of the situation regarding the express passenger stock in the early days of the Southern, Maunsell then instigated some investigations to check the viability of certain modifications to the draughting and valve travel to overcome the shortcomings of these 4-6-0s. Concurrently, Clayton was given the responsibility for the task of preparing the 'N15' design for future production, the need for express types being so pressing that a new design could not be carried out in the time allotted. The main modifications Clayton designed in, based on the tests carried out on Maunsell's instructions, consisted of revising the draughting along the lines of that adopted for the 'N' class, increasing the boiler pressure from 180 lb./sq.in. to 200 lb./sq.in, reducing the cylinder diameter from 22 in. to 20½ in., increasing the valve travel and providing increased airflow through the ashpan. With these changes, the 'N15' new production became the 'King Arthur' class, to be the mainstay of Southern express services on all Sections until the advent of Bulleid's 'Merchant Navy', 'West Country' and 'Battle of Britain' Pacifics of the mid-to-late 1940s.

It was the tests of the improved draughting that produced the most effective cure to the steaming problems, so even before the first 'King Arthur' appeared in 1925, success was assured. The class eventually totalled 74 in number, comprising 20 rebuilds of Urie 'N15s' and three batches of 10, 30 and 14, the first batch from Eastleigh, the second from the North British Locomotive Company, both in 1925, and the third from Eastleigh in 1926. The last two batches had Ashford cabs which conformed to the Southern composite

Urie 'N15' No. 453, *King Arthur* in person, before the installation of smoke deflectors.

Maunsell 'N15' No. 788 *Sir Urre of the Mount*. A 'Scotch' Arthur employing the modified cab and Urie tender.

MLS Collection

An Eastleigh 'N15' No. 796 *Sir Dodinas le Savage* with a 6-wheel tender on a Margate Express.

Real Photographs

loading gauge. The 1926 batch were provided with 6-wheel tenders to permit their employment on the Central (Brighton) Section, which had restricted turntable sizes.

Incidentally, the 'King Arthurs' were the first named locomotives on the Southern Railway, although the LB&SCR had, for many years, instituted such a policy. The naming resulted from a suggestion from John Elliot, the then Public Relations Assistant to Sir Herbert Walker, that express trains warranted locomotives named after personalities and places associated with King Arthur, the legends of whom were connected to the area served by the Western Section of the Southern. Walker asked Elliot to suggest this to Maunsell, who had no objection but did make the comment: 'I warn you it won't make any difference to the working of the engine!'

From the earliest days at Waterloo, Maunsell requested that all important drawings from Eastleigh were vetted and passed to him for final signature. 'Jock' Finlayson and his immediate team tended to drift back to Urie's methodology and needed firm restraining at times, and this was the best way in which to prevent the older methods being infiltrated into designs. Richard had his own ideas and plans as to which way he wanted things done and dictated this by his firm handling of this situation. Had the changes requested on some drawings come from others, such as Holcroft or Clayton, Finlayson would, and indeed did, try to ignore them if they went against his own personal traits. However, the personal authority of the CME was enough to bend his will and make him accept the rulings laid down. Richard was clearly in touch with events and meant to exert his will when needed.

Eastleigh also provided further problems in the shape of Surrey Warner, who appeared at Waterloo complaining about the activities of the Waterloo team, particularly the appearance of 'brass hats', as he termed them, without any prior arrangement or warning. Maunsell managed to calm him down, taking the blame on his own shoulders and promising that in future, all visits would be notified beforehand and an agreed procedure of announcing the arrival at Eastleigh premises was set up.

About this time, it came to the notice of Maunsell that some weighing data for some of the larger engines at Eastleigh had been derived from conditions not consistent with that of having full water in the boiler and coal on the grate. This had been done deliberately in order to show no more than the Engineer's limit of 20 tons axle loading. At this revelation he was extremely angry, it was his practice not to accept the slightest deviation from the truth and requested that all the weighings involved should be redone with the chief draughtsman present and the revised data submitted to Waterloo for his perusal. Those involved were warned of serious consequences should any further inaccuracies arise.

Concurrent to all this, Richard was busily employed in the design of the 'Lord Nelson' class, more developments of the successful Moguls, the introduction of the 'River' class express tanks (of which more later) and the provision of some extra 4-4-0s based on Wainwright's 'L' class. Times were busy in the Drawing Offices as the Southern locomotive scene settled down and adjusted to cope with the onset of expansion into electrification, which was shortly to be

'L1' No. 788.   *H.M. Dannatt Collection*

The great little 4-4-0, the 'L1' class developed by Maunsell, at Tonbridge 20th September, 1947.
J.M. Jarvis Collection

accelerated following the Board's acceptance of the recommendations of the Cox Committee's investigation into the preferred method and type of current supply.

The extra 4-4-0s mentioned above formed the 'L1'class. Although based on the 'L', these locomotives were a completely new build, and emanated from a request from the Traffic Department for more 'Ls' to cope with the London-Folkestone boat trains. However, Maunsell took stock of the situation, in that these trains were already approaching weights where the standard 'L' class was finding it difficult to maintain the tight timing associated with them. He accordingly set about modifying the design of the 'L' to include increased boiler pressure, from 160 lb./sq. in. to 180 lb./sq. in.; the cylinders were reduced in diameter, from 20½ in. to 19 in.; the valve travel was also increased considerably. Structurally, the new 4-4-0 was similar to the 'D1' and 'E1' rebuilds, with the raised running plate over the coupled wheels. The smokebox and chimney was taken from the 'N' to incorporate its excellent draughting. Maunsell specified his own superheater design, and the cab was given side windows, the first of his designs so fitted. Fifteen were authorised and built by the North British Locomotive Company in 1926.

The resulting locomotive was an immediate success, and the boat trains were assured of the necessary time-keeping. In later years when the unique 'Night Ferry' train of heavy sleeping cars between London and Paris commenced, it was the 'L1' which became the regular motive power, albeit with double-heading. This unique combination was to last, apart for the War years, until the early days of British Railways, when the Bulleid Light Pacifics took over. But even then an 'L1' was often to be found double-heading the Pacific! The large steam heating demands of the sleeping cars called for the extra engine.

So, with the express and boat train needs being satisfied with modifications to the best of the designs of Maunsell's predecessors, the Southern was ready to assimilate the future planned locomotives to issue from the Drawing Offices.

One little episode in Maunsell's life which has survived the passage of time concerns the Railway Centenary celebrations held at Darlington on 1st to 3rd July, 1925, to which many delegates from the 10th International Railway Congress, held at the Institution of Civil Engineers and timed to coincide with this historic event, travelled for the celebrations. This event was hosted by the LNER and Maunsell was one of the 700 who were to attend. In typical railway fashion, there was a big banquet associated with this gathering, held in the Paint Shop of the Darlington Works. Maunsell sat at a table with Gresley, Stamer, Thompson, Harper, Wilson, Watson and Gibb. The first three were, or were to be, top Mechanical Engineers, Gresley to be succeeded on his death by Thompson, and Stamer was to retire in 1933 from his Assistant CME post at Darlington. Of the remainder, Alex Wilson was LNER Southern Area General Manager, A.H. Watson the former General Superintendent of the North Eastern Railway (NER), J.B. Harper the former Assistant General Superintendent of the NER and Paul Gibb, son of Sir George Gibb, was assistant to the Divisional General Manager, Southern Area, LNER. Maunsell kept the menu cover from

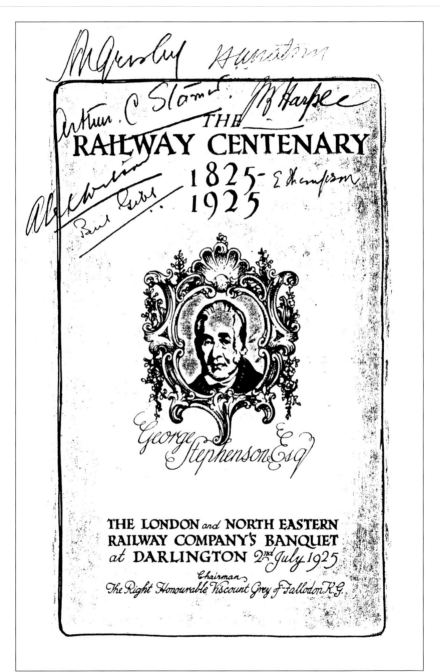

Centenary Banquet Menu cover with signatures obtained by Maunsell from his table
companions.   *G.M. Rial*

this banquet, having had it signed by all the persons mentioned, as a memento of this memorable event. This has survived in private hands and there is a copy in the National Railway Museum archives (*see illustration opposite*). During the Darlington celebrations there was a parade of locomotives, some with complete trains, going back to the *Locomotion* of the Stockton and Darlington Railway of 1925, up to the latest in motive power from the four main groups. The Southern was represented by 'N15' class No. E449, *Sir Torre*, fresh from the production line at Eastleigh, pulling a restaurant car set of the latest new design of carriages.

There was plenty of other work on top of the demands for new locomotives needing Maunsell's attention during the early years of the Southern. Much of this was associated with modifications to existing classes. As Grouping happened the Brighton works was busily engaged on the 'B4X' rebuild exercise covering 12 of the 33-strong class, although perhaps the term 'rebuild' was there for the benefit of the accountants. The 'B4X' was derived from the dated Billinton 'B4' class, but little of the original locomotive remained save the wheels, bogies and motion. The boilers were replaced with those similar to the class 'K' Mogul, new cabs were fitted, and the tender was modified to take 3,600 gallons from the earlier 3,000 gallon of the 'B4'. Although the end result was a sturdy looking engine, their performance was never sparkling. However, Holcroft did assess this type during his footplate trips and made the comment that given long travel valves they would have been very good mid-range express types. On the freight side, Urie had started to superheat the Drummond '700' class 'Black Motors'. Maunsell continued this exercise to completion of the whole class, even going as far as changing the Eastleigh type of superheater for his own design in the process. Continuing in the exercises to update and improve existing classes, five of the ex-LB&SCR 'I3' tanks were superheated. This completed the 1923 list.

In 1925, the 'Black Motors' were still undergoing the superheating programme, which was now extended to Drummond 'L12s' and 'T9s', plus the 'H1' Atlantics, involving some 91 locomotives in total. One considerable rebuild exercise which commenced this year involved the Marsh 'I1' 4-4-2 tanks, which were notoriously bad steamers. These were fitted with 'B4' type boilers and 'River' class cabs to improve their usefulness. The whole class was rebuilt thus, in stages, being completed by 1931.

The final major rebuild took place in 1927, this being the conversion of 10 class 'E1' 0-6-0 tanks to 'E1R' 0-6-2 tanks. The increase in bunker and water capacity required the extra carrying wheels which were provided by using the 'N' class radial pony truck, which was obtained from spares manufactured for the 'N' class Mogul.

It was also noticed by Maunsell, on his many visits to the works, that much siding space in the vicinity of the works was occupied by dead locomotives awaiting repair. Realising from past experience that congested sidings in the vicinity of works could cause delays in moving stock around between the various shops, he ordered that such locomotives be kept at their home sheds until it was known when they would be able to enter the works directly.

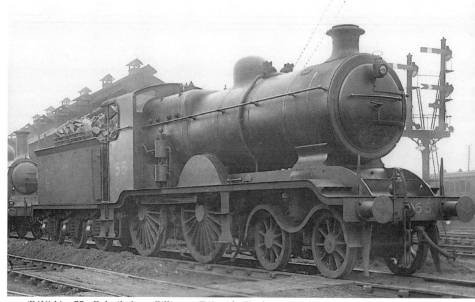

'B4X' No. 55. Rebuilt from Billinton 'B4' with 'K' class 2-6-0 boiler. In original condition with Billinton top feed.   *H.M. Dannatt Collection*

'I1X' No. 595. Reboilered by Maunsell using surplus boilers from the 'B4' rebuilds.
                                                                                          H.M. Dannatt Collection

So, we see that Richard was very busy indeed in the early years of the Southern's existence, and had certainly made his mark on the locomotive scene. All too often, we tend to relate all designs, whether improvements, rebuilds or new, to the CME himself. This is incorrect, as the job of CME covers such a wide range of disciplines, from initial design through to in-service operation of, not only the locomotives, but also the rolling stock. Much of the effort put into design changes and improvements would have been delegated down through the team at Waterloo. Maunsell was renowned as a first-class delegator, and it is obvious from a study of the programme of locomotive, carriage and wagon work carried out throughout his sojourn in the position of CME, that his choice of and guidance to the engineering staff ensured that this extensive programme was carried out so efficiently and quickly.

Meanwhile, we must go back to earlier times on the GS&WR and SE&CR to cover the story of the development of the Moguls.

The 'E1R' 0-6-2 tank, No. B124.   *Real Photographs*

'N' class No. 1403. This was of the final 1932 batch, and is in 'as-built' condition, before the smoke deflectors were fitted in 1933, and appears to have steam to spare for the heavy freight in its charge.   *MLS Collection*

The footplate and backhead of preserved 'N' class No. 1874.   *Author*

Chapter Seven

The Moguls
The Maids-of-all-Work

By the early days of World War I it had become clear that the SE&CR required to add to its stud of 4-4-0 and 0-6-0 tender locomotives, and this was the first major design task that Maunsell faced at Ashford. A 2-6-0, or Mogul, was proposed as the obvious solution for a versatile engine to cater for both passenger and freight traffic. The Mogul first appeared in the United States in the 1890s and, indeed, had been so successful there that some had been imported by the Midland, Great Central and Great Northern Railways. Some engineers looked upon this development as an undesirable intrusion into British locomotive practice. However, following the introduction of Churchward's '43XX' class on the Great Western, the virtues of this layout were apparent for all to see and further indigenous examples appeared on the LB&SC, Great Northern, Caledonian and Glasgow & South Western Railways.

Richard Maunsell was not inexperienced in the 2-6-0 wheel arrangement, and we need to go back to his Inchicore days to discuss this. It is generally assumed that the SE&CR 'N' class was his first brush with the Mogul. Not so, for whilst at Inchicore, during his Works Manager days, he had been involved in the design and construction of two batches of freight locomotives of this type.

The first batch, the '355' class, came about by a need to rebuild six 0-6-0s built in 1903 which had excessive weight on the front coupled wheels (the GS&WR was still limited to 15 tons axle loading over much of the secondary lines) which restricted their route availability. Accordingly these were withdrawn in 1907 for modifications incorporating a set of radial front carrying wheels to alleviate the axle loading problem. The second batch, class '368', had significant changes in that a larger boiler was employed and the Mogul arrangement was standard from the start. It also was the first Inchicore design to employ a Belpaire firebox, so popular with Richard in later years. Four were constructed in 1909, and are the ones mentioned in Chapter Two. All these Coey 2-6-0s had inside cylinders.

Maunsell accordingly placed the requirement for a new six-coupled mixed-traffic locomotive with his team at Ashford. And so began the Mogul story which eventually was, on the SE&CR and Southern, to result in 157 engines of four classes over the 1917 to 1934 time span.

The prototype 2-6-0, which appeared in 1917, was to be the forerunner of the 'N' class, numerically the largest of the four classes. The primary duty envisaged was for heavy freight trains of up to 1,000 tons between Ashford and Hither Green, Ramsgate and Dover. Maunsell, due to his preoccupation in War work for the Railway Executive Committee, left the detail design to Clayton, who was advised by Holcroft and Pearson, with the proviso that everything had to be 'get-at-able'. It had been Holcroft who had convinced Maunsell of the virtues of the Great Western approach to the 2-6-0, based on his earlier Swindon involvement in the design of the '43XX' class, of which many hundreds were to be produced over the years. And so it was hardly surprising that the result was

Ashford New Erecting Shop, 11th September, 1937. Several Moguls are to be seen undergoing heavy repairs.
Ray Elam

'N' class No. 1834, at an unknown location, *c*. 1939.
MLS Collection

almost pure Swindon, with long-travel piston valves, Belpaire firebox, tapered boiler and wheel size very similar to the Great Western Moguls. One other typical Swindon feature was the steam collection via a perforated pipe in the top corner of the firebox, the dome being purely for the boiler top-feed apparatus. However, there was one departure from current Swindon practice, specified by Maunsell, with the higher degree of superheat than that prevalent on the GWR. The one distinctive visible feature not in line with Great Western practice, which resulted from Maunsell's ease of access dictum, was the employment of outside Walschaerts' gear as against the inside Stephenson gear widely employed by the GWR.

This one basic design was to form the starting point not only for three other classes but also the ill-fated 'River' class tanks and the later 'W' class tanks. The main feature common to all was the smokebox/boiler/firebox assembly. The full story of the 'River' tanks is contained in the next chapter.

As has been indicated earlier, the 'N' class was the most prolific of Maunsell's Moguls and certainly unique in that it was also employed on the Great Southern Railway of Ireland. The reason for this latter was due to the fact that, following World War I, the Woolwich Arsenal was saved from stagnation and large lay-offs caused by the sudden end of the need for munitions by Winston Churchill, then Minister of Munitions, who conceived the idea of employing this large plant in the production of locomotives. There was, he reasoned, a clear case for the production of new and replacement engines to make up the deficits caused by arrears of production at the British railway works, which had been diverting effort to aid war production of heavy machinery and munitions. There was also an underlying political reason for such mass production, this being the current Government thinking of Nationalisation of the railway system. Standard designs would be required in large numbers. However it proved difficult to decide which type should be built, and the British railways were reluctant to take locomotives constructed at a plant with no previous history of such production.

Maunsell's time as Chief Mechanical Engineer to the Railway Executive Committee during the War meant that he was well respected in Ministry circles and, eventually he was persuaded to permit 100 of his 'N' class to be built at Woolwich Arsenal. As had been vainly pointed out, no takers were to be found, and the Government found itself with 100 locomotives on its hands. In despair a few examples were sent to Ashford for assessment. Their condition was far from ideal, due largely to the inexperience of Woolwich, and required considerable attention, almost a complete rebuild, before being released into service. In view of this, Maunsell was eventually persuaded to make an offer for 50 examples at a price which was far below the value of the locomotives and which was eventually accepted. The listing of these engines shows a combined Woolwich Arsenal and Ashford source of supply, so it appears that the whole 50 were rebuilt at Ashford in order to eliminate the endemic problems. A further 15 'N' class locomotives, Nos. 1400 to 1414, were built at Ashford in 1932-1934. See *Table Three* for a summary of the dates and numbers into service.

Of the remaining 35 examples, 27 were taken by the Great Southern Railway in Ireland (GSR (I))and erected at their Broadstone works, being regauged to

5 ft 3 in. in the process, so Maunsell at last had a further example of his design expertise at work in his native country. Being the most powerful locomotives in service and remaining thus until the introduction of the '800' class 4-6-0 in 1939, they soon became the premier type on the Midland Great Western section of the GSR (I), in addition being employed for the Cork and Rosslare boat trains, which was over a particularly difficult route. See *Table Two* for a summary of these Irish examples, which were the only new types to enter service on this railway in the first 14 years following its creation in 1925. As a matter of interest the price was a mere £2,000 each, a bargain!

Table Two

The Maunsell Moguls (GSR (I))

GSR Class	Built at	Year	Number
K1	Woolwich Arsenal/Broadstone	1925	2
K1	Woolwich Arsenal/Broadstone	1926	8
K1	Woolwich Arsenal/Broadstone	1927	5
K1	Woolwich Arsenal/Broadstone	1928	3
K1	Woolwich Arsenal/Broadstone	1929	2
K1A	Woolwich Arsenal/Broadstone	1930	6 *

Notes: * This batch with 6 ft diameter coupled wheels.
NB   27 sets of parts were purchased, but one complete set was retained for spares.

Of the remaining eight 'Ns' produced at Woolwich six were taken up, as a series of parts, by the Metropolitan Railway for use in constructing some 2-6-4 tanks.

The first recorded use of the 'N' class for experimental purposes was in 1924, when No. A818 was fitted with a Worthington feed pump to assess the potential of this apparatus. Many of the ex-Brighton locomotives had employed Weir feed pumps for many years and Richard was interested in comparing the Worthington system with a view to its adoption. However, the results indicated no distinct advantage in efficiency or cost, and No. A818 reverted back to the standard injectors after 2½ years.

One particular experimental episode of note involving another example of the 'N' class took place shortly after the feed pump experiment. On 24th November 1927, Maunsell called Holcroft into a meeting, at which he was asked to go to the City offices of the Steam Heat Conservation Company to collect information on the Anderson system of condensing and returning exhaust steam as feed water to the boiler of a locomotive. The data provided gave promise of considerable fuel savings and, accordingly, Holcroft was given authority to proceed in November 1928. Eastleigh was given the responsibility of producing the necessary drawings, which were completed in January 1930. 'N' class No. A816 was allocated for the testing and was modified to take the system as designed. It was a semi-condensing system, employing a fan-induced draught provided by a rotary steam engine driving a fan in the smokebox door and duplicated condensing gear with feed pumps each side of the running plate. The resulting modified locomotive was a bit of an eyesore, with apparatus cluttering up the running plate, and was employed on trials for about two years. The results, after some early setbacks with equipment, were encouraging, but towards the end of this time the makers of the system ran out of money, and the project died. One notable feature of this engine was its almost total absence of noise under power.

One further use of one of the 'N' class, No. 1850, for experimental purposes was in 1934, when it was fitted with a complex valve gear devised by James Marshall, who was connected to the Gainsborough agricultural engineering family. Marshall and Maunsell had collaborated back in 1904, when an earlier version of Marshall's valve gear had been tried out in comparative trials, on Coey 4-4-0 No. 307 at Inchicore. The Mogul trials, as with the earlier Inchicore tests, did not result in any further employment of the Marshall gear, and the locomotive reverted to its original form at the end of the trials.

The first iteration on the Mogul theme came in December 1922, with the 'N1' class, the prototype of which appeared under the SE&CR auspices, and ranks as the last locomotive built for that company. The smallest numbered class of any of Maunsell's designs, a mere six were eventually to enter traffic.

We have already seen in Chapter Three that Maunsell had indicated a leaning towards employing conjugated valve gear for three-cylinder locomotives when at Inchicore on his 0-8-2T project study. The opportunity to pursue this method of valve operation on such types presented itself when the prototype 'N1' Mogul was being designed. The fact that Holcroft had also proposed developing a conjugated gear, coupled with Richard's earlier Inchicore episode, indicates a willingness to pursue development work through to an ultimate conclusion. Many lesser men would have dismissed the idea after the first failure. The engineering expertise shows through here.

The 'N1' evolved from an exercise to develop a three-cylinder version of the 'N', and the prototype employed the rather ungainly looking, but simple Holcroft conjugated gear, whereby a linkage from the two outside sets of Walschaerts' gear, which passed by the outside of the valve casing, drove the valve for the inside cylinder through a couple of pivoting cranks, identical in concept to that employed by Gresley on the GNR 'K3' Mogul of 1920. However, it is perhaps worth pointing out here that Holcroft's conjugated gear involvement dated back to his days at Swindon in 1909, where he designed a version of it. Churchward, ever mindful of covering new ideas, instructed him to patent it, which he duly instigated, only to find in the search procedure that David Joy had some years previously applied for a Patent involving conjugated gear for a triple expansion marine engine. The Holcroft proposal was therefore not proceeded with. But shortly after this the Great Western had decided to settle for the four-cylinder layout for express locomotives and, apparently, the possibilities of taking the application further was not of interest to the GWR, so Holcroft was perfectly in order to propose it for employment on the prototype three-cylinder Mogul.

Its use was relatively shortlived on the 'N1', due to the fact that the whip found on the rather long and slim drive shafts at high speed tended to cause over-run on the centre valve, a problem that was said to beset the Gresley three-cylinder designs for many years. Properly maintained, conjugated gear is

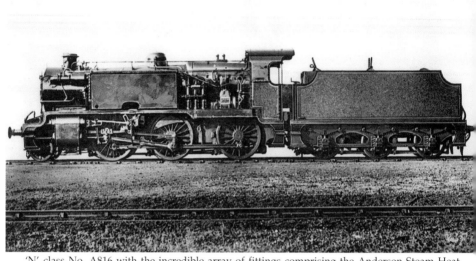

'N' class No. A816 with the incredible array of fittings comprising the Anderson Steam Heat Conservation system tested between 1932 and 1934.   *H.M. Dannatt Collection*

'N' class No. 1850 fitted with indicator shelters for the series of tests with the Marshall valve gear.   *MLS Collection*

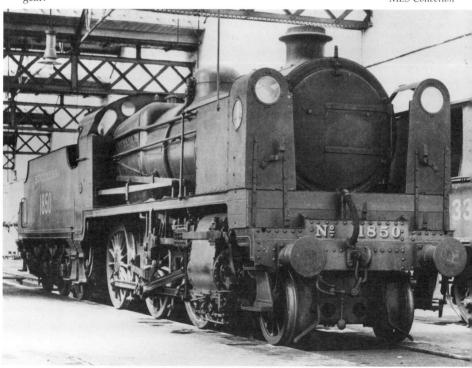

perfectly satisfactory, but such maintenance was at intervals which did not necessarily line up with the normal schedules. The large clearances required on the conjugated gear pin joints were dictated by the need to cover for inaccuracies in the erection of the locomotives, which were prevalent with the level of technology available at that time. More modern techniques now available, involving lining up of structures with Laser beams, would permit closer tolerances to be achieved.

Before the production batch of five appeared, which was not until 1930, it had already been decided to modify the prototype with a centre set of Walschaerts' gear. Needless to say, these five followed suit from their inception. However, the original conjugated gear concept was responsible for the distinctive inset position of the outside cylinder valve chests on all three-cylinder versions of the Mogul which lived on after its reversion to the centre eccentric, it being uneconomic to change the tooling. The 'Z' and 'W' class tanks, also three-cylindered, employed the same outside cylinder castings as the 'N1', and thus had this distinctive feature, even though they were never produced with conjugated gear.

One fact concerning Gresley's adoption of a conjugated gear for three-cylinder designs was that, during the early days of Holcroft's schemes for his approach to the problem he (Holcroft), as mentioned earlier in Chapter Five, had talked with Gresley, whom he knew favoured this type of locomotive. The early Gresley scheme was very complex, having no less than 11 pin joints, whereas Holcroft achieved the same motion with just eight. An even simpler five-pin arrangement was then developed by Gresley to alleviate complaints regarding excessive wear liable to appear on his 11 pin-joint design. It was during this time that he had the discussion with Holcroft who showed his schemes which enabled this gear to be fitted to an inclined inside cylinder, thus permitting the drive to be concentrated on one axle, which Gresley always preferred. Acknowledgement to Holcroft's involvement in this design exercise was given, in that the early publications on the gear referred to it as the Gresley-Holcroft system. Yet the article on the 'N1' design published in *The Engineer* of 23rd February, 1923, specifically refers to the actuation of the middle cylinder valve as being by 'a modified Gresley gear . . .' However, it is worth noting that whilst Gresley persisted in his conjugated gear for the rest of his career, Maunsell quickly realised the possible problems of wear and whip of the Holcroft scheme affecting locomotive performance, and decided to revert to the more conventional Walschaerts' eccentric for the inside cylinder on all his three-cylinder designs.

The next Mogul class to appear, was the 'U'. This particular version appeared as a result of the 'River' class tank rebuilds, ordered after the Sevenoaks accident. A further order for another batch of these tanks had been placed some time prior to this disaster, but had already been converted to 2-6-0 tender types and the first of them were actually under construction, for reasons to be explained in the next chapter.

Conversion of the tanks was required as speedily as possible to minimise any disruption caused by the sudden withdrawal of top link express types, thus Ashford, Brighton and Eastleigh were all involved, with Brighton and Ashford

'W' class No. 1631 hauling a substantial freight.

catering for the new builds, which totalled 30 in number. There was one feature of the 'U' class which departed from the standards enjoyed by the earlier 'N', this being the coupled wheel diameter of 6 ft, as against 5 ft 6 in. of the latter. As a result, the 'Us' tended to be regarded more as passenger types, rather than the mixed traffic mode of the 'N'. One minor detail point which identified the 'U', both the rebuilds and those new, was the retention of the 7 ft 9 in. wheelbase between the centre and rear wheels which had been that of the tanks, as compared to the 8 ft 3 in. common to the earlier tender types.

In 1929, Maunsell ordered that some experiments into the use of pulverised coal be carried out. Accordingly, 'U' class No. A629 was built with the apparatus to burn this type of fuel, and ran until 1932 in this form. Plant for producing this form of fuel, supplied by AEG of Germany, was set up at Eastbourne shed. Experience in Germany and New South Wales with this form of fuel had been quite encouraging, but therein lay the difference, they had used soft brown coal which was easy to crush into powdered form. The harder coal used by the railways in Britain, whilst crushable, was liable to produce lumps which jammed the mechanism for feeding it into the firebox. The extra trouble caused by this outweighed the cost advantages of being able to use lower grade fuel and the experiment terminated.

The single example of the 3-cylinder version of the 'River' class tank was rebuilt as the prototype of the 'U1' class, retaining the Holcroft conjugated valve gear and the 7 ft 9 in. centre wheelbase of the tank. As with the 'N1' class, the conjugated gear was eventually replaced by a centre Walschaerts' gear, and when the production batch of 20 appeared in 1931, they were fitted thus. Although Ashford was responsible for the rebuild, all the production engines were erected at Eastleigh. In 1928, prior to the clearance for production of the 'U1', a study involving a further variant of this model had been carried out. This project was for a reduced width 'U1' specifically for the Hastings line, with its limited tunnel clearance restrictions. However, shortly after the drawings had been schemed, the 'Schools' class was in planning, and effectively removed the need for this Mogul variant. Additionally, some trials of a representative of this class were made on that line which showed that the flange wear on the leading coupled wheels to be excessive due to the numerous curves on this difficult route.

Until the beginning of the withdrawal of steam on British Railways in the early 1960s, the Maunsell Moguls were to be found on passenger and freight work all over the Southern area. Versatile and reliable locomotives, they dealt with much of the run-of-the-mill Southern movements, the mundane stopping passenger, goods services, and cross-country trains that were the backbone of railway services. However, they were also frequently to be found on excursions and specials at weekends, and to all accounts, performed well on demanding schedules. What better epitaph could a well-balanced design give to its instigator?

Table Three, listing of all the Maunsell Moguls built by the SE&CR and Southern, is included here to summarise the classes and numbers of each class that entered service over the years between introduction and final production.

'U1' prototype No. 890, as converted from the sole 'K1' tank. Initially this engine retained the
Holcroft gear.   *Author's Collection*

'U1' class No. 1909, as built, before smoke deflectors were fitted, which places this picture in the
early 1930s.   *MLS Collection*

Table Three

The Maunsell Moguls

Class	Built at	Year	Number	Notes
N	Ashford	1917	1	(P)
N	Ashford	1920	5	
N	Ashford	1922-3	9	
	Woolwich Arsenal/Ashford	1924	20	
	Woolwich Arsenal/Ashford	1925	30	
	Ashford	1932	6	
	Ashford	1933	7	
	Ashford	1934	2	
N1	Ashford	1922	1	(P)
N1	Ashford	1930	5	
U	Eastleigh	1928	7	*
U	Ashford	1928	9	†
U	Brighton	1928	16	#
U	Ashford	1929	8	
U	Ashford	1931	10	
U1	Ashford	1928	1	* (P)
U1	Eastleigh	1931	20	

Notes: (P)   Denotes prototype.
          *   Rebuilt from 'River' class tanks.
          †   Seven of this batch rebuilt from 'River' tanks.
          #   Six of this batch rebuilt from 'River' tanks.

'U1' class No. 31890 in BR days leaving Tonbridge yard on a down freight.

MLS Collection

The largest example of a passenger tank when Maunsell arrived at Ashford was Wainwright's 0-6-4T, class 'J', of which No. 1596 is seen here at Ashford on 12th July, 1939.

John P. Wilson/Rail Archive Stephenson

'K' class 2-6-4T No. 793 *River Ouse* preparing to leave Victoria with one of the Brighton expresses.   This was one of the batch built by Armstrong-Whitworth and fitted with Westinghouse pumps for the Brighton line services.   *H.M. Dannatt Collection*

Chapter Eight

Tank Engines and the Sevenoaks Incidents

The LB&SCR, one of the constituent companies that made up the Southern Railway at Grouping, had had a history of using express tank locomotives quite extensively on its main lines since 1908, and it could well have been that Maunsell had been influenced by their success when putting forward the proposal to provide the 'River' class 2-6-4T for such a duty. Tank engines take up less platform space in crowded city terminals, can show economies in construction and servicing, should not require turning at the end of each journey, but have the restriction of limited range due to their low water capacity. The LB&SCR main line run to Brighton was merely 60 miles, within the range of tank locomotives, and this was the reason why they had been so successfully employed on express work. Although it should be stated that the large 'L' class 4-6-4 tanks introduced by L.B. Billinton in 1914, of which an initial two were built, had been prone to unsteady riding at speed. There was a derailment due to this on the main line at Hassocks which was traced to water surging in the tanks at speed. This was cured by fitting a well tank between the frames under the boiler and allowing this to reduce the water level in the side tanks substantially, thus lowering the centre of gravity, which proved successful enough to permit the construction of a further five in 1921-2. All seven of these engines entered Southern usage after Grouping, and were employed in their original form until rebuilding as tender types in 1934-36. There were a further two express 4-6-2 tanks of LB&SCR vintage, Marsh's class 'J', which survived as built, apart from limited changes to permit their use on other sections of the Southern, until withdrawal in 1951.

The former SE&CR main lines on the Eastern section were, on the whole, longer than their LB&SCR equivalents, and even with modern tank locomotives, the maximum range was limited by their water capacity under normal usage. Several of the expresses that the tanks were employed on had a booked stop at around 60 miles, to take on water, because of this. So, bearing in mind the operational advantages, it was not difficult to understand Maunsell's acceptance of the reasoning behind the employment of tank locomotives for such purposes, providing that the restrictions imposed by limited range were acceptable to the operating department. His decision was also backed by the encouragement of George Pearson to consider large tank engines in the early days at Ashford.

So, with the promising results from tests on the prototype 'K' class tank, Maunsell was authorised to provide 20 more in 1922. Due to pressure of work at Ashford, nine were erected by Armstrong Whitworth at Newcastle-upon-Tyne from parts manufactured and supplied by Ashford. These examples were fitted with Westinghouse pumps for service on the Brighton lines. Ten more were built at Brighton, with the sole remaining example being built at Ashford. This last one was the three-cylinder variant, class 'K1', later to become the prototype for the future class 'U1' Mogul, and was fitted with Holcroft's conjugated valve gear.

'K1' class 3-cylinder 2-6-4 tank No. 890 *River Frome*.

All entered traffic and were giving good account of themselves on the Eastern and Central sections, but some disconcerting reports of rough riding were beginning to be heard, and then, on 20th August, 1927, No. 890 the prototype three-cylinder tank and its train were completely derailed just past Bearsted station. The train in question was the 10.51 am Charing Cross to Margate and the estimated speed at the point of derailment just 40 mph. The driver had not noticed any particularly bad oscillation just prior to the incident. The riding suddenly became rough as the leading coupled wheels left the rails followed immediately by the remaining coupled wheels and rear bogie wheels. The resulting damage to the track was such that the remainder of the train progressively derailed as it was successfully brought to a halt in 166 yards, until just a van bringing up the rear of the formation plus the rear bogie of the last coach remained on the track. No one was injured in the rather bumpy ride and sharp deceleration.

No. 890 had, up to now, had the reputation of being a rough rider, worse in fact than the two-cylinder versions in service. At the inquiry held as a result of this derailment, it was stated that just 18 minutes prior to the passage of No. 890, 'E' class No. 587 had passed over the track in question and the crew stated that they could remember nothing notable about the riding characteristics encountered in that area. However, one reason was raised as being a contributory cause, this being the loading per foot run over the coupled wheels of the 'E' and 'K1' classes. For the former it was 3.52 tons/ft and the latter 3.22 tons/ft. A very similar value of rail pressure, which it was thought may have resulted in enough movement being generated to cause the water in the half empty tanks to surge excessively and compound the oscillatory forces, which somehow grew to a sufficient extent such that the leading coupled wheels climbed over the rail so setting off the chain of events. The mark of this wheel's flange on the rail top surface was clearly visible at the point of initial derailment. All the available evidence pointed towards a deficiency in the track bed causing excessive rail depression under normal loading. The passage of the 'E' and its train a few minutes before No. 890 could have caused subsidence in the track bringing about a lurch which precipitated the surging in the tanks, enough to cause the pony truck to derail. This is pure speculation, but does appear to be a logical reason for the derailment.

By the time the analysis of this event was under way, disaster struck. On the 24th August, to an express from Cannon Street to Folkestone, hauled by one of the tanks, No. 800 *River Cray*, was derailed at speed on the down gradient from Polhill to Sevenoaks. Thirteen passengers were killed, with 21 more seriously injured in the ensuing crash, which blocked both lines. Again, the locomotive started the chain of events.

Maunsell, at the time of the accident, was on holiday in Rome with Edith, staying at the Hotel Hassler and New York, and had to be located and recalled in order to be available for the official inquiry that was immediately set up.

Following this second accident and the receipt of the official report, Sir Herbert Walker, the Southern Railway General Manager, called a special meeting of the Chief Officers involved and some of the following comments are taken verbatim from Sir John Elliot's account of the meeting, at which he was

Sevenoaks crash. 'K' class tank No. 800 *River Cray* lies on its side in the cutting about 100 yards past the bridge. Note the location of the front pony truck, under the front drivers, and the telescoped front coach.   *Wakeman Collection, Ashford Library*

A view from the up side of the bridge showing the Pullman car jammed across the track. Just beyond this is the coach which initially jammed into the bridge. The weight of the Pullman car and the impact of the rear of the train on the jammed coach reduced it to matchwood. It was here that the majority of the fatal injuries occurred.   *Wakeman Collection, Ashford Library*

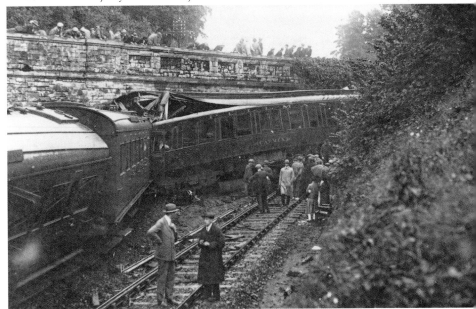

present: 'We have had a serious accident', began Sir Herbert Walker, 'Something is wrong somewhere'. Turning to Maunsell, he said, 'Do you suspect that your tank locomotive became unstable? If not, what?'

Maunsell replied, 'The locomotive is perfectly stable. It has been run at high speeds on other main lines and I can only conclude that the fault lies with the track'.

Turning then to George Ellson, the Chief Civil Engineer, Walker said, 'Well, Ellson, what is your view?'

This was a difficult moment for Ellson, who had only recently taken over his engineering responsibilities. Based on visits made to the site with his officers, he replied that no evidence could be found that the track was at fault.

The classic impasse of Ellson and Maunsell both denying that their particular sphere was not to blame was resolved by Walker, who stated that in his opinion the combination of track condition and the locomotive's propensity to ride roughly could well be the root of the problem. The 'River' class tanks were immediately withdrawn from service and, as Walker had actually intimated during the meeting, eventually rebuilt as tender types. Subsequently, the report of the official inquiry did state that the track had been affected by a cloudburst on the morning of the accident and that the locomotives were prone to rolling, due to surging of the water in the tanks. As Sir Herbert had indicated, the combination of these factors proved fatal on that day, in that the leading coupled wheels and, subsequently, the front pony truck were derailed by the reaction of the locomotive's rolling caused by uneven track at the south end of Dunton Green station. The derailed pony truck, after travelling some 500 yards in that condition, then burst a pair of trailing catch points, following which the engine and train were completely derailed. The driver, realising that the rough riding was persisting and suspecting something more serious, had closed the regulator and applied the brake fully, but to no avail. With the train travelling at 60 mph, there was little chance of any significant speed reduction being made. To further complicate matters, the derailed engine slewed round and struck the side of a bridge, which threw it on its side. Two coaches went through the bridge with the engine, but the third coach became detached from the fourth and jammed under the bridge, being very severely crushed. The remaining coaches piled up against the wreckage and bridge causing many of the deaths and injuries.

Trials that were carried out on the 'River' class tanks on both the LNER and the Southern to assess their stability resulted in some anomalous results. In respect of the trials on the LNER the tanks acquitted themselves well, even when running backwards at speeds in excess of 80 mph. The corresponding Southern trials, however, were a different tale, the rolling being considered excessive at high speeds. It all boiled down to the relative states of the track, on the LNER the condition of which was much superior to that of the Southern. In the end, although the culprit was undoubtedly the standard of the Southern track, there seemed no point in having an engine which only rode well on perfectly maintained track if there was no such track to run on. Hence the wisdom of Sir Herbert Walker's statement regarding conversion of the (admittedly handsome) 'River' class tanks, of which there were 21 examples in

Baltic tank No. 2331 before conversion to a 4-6-0 tender type. Certainly there is no indication that a well tank rests between the frames. The side tanks were never filled more than a quarter full (drawings indicate baffles to prevent over-filling). This ensured that water surging was insufficient to accentuate the rolling at speed.   *H.M. Dannatt Collection*

The Maunsell conversion of the Billinton 4-6-4 express tank. Class 'N15X' No. 2329 *Stephenson* in photographic grey.   *MLS Collection*

service. The prototype dated from the SE&CR six-coupled exercise of 1917, the remainder being constructed in 1925-6. The 20 two-cylinder versions became part of the 'U' class of 2-6-0 tender locomotives, whilst the single three-cylinder version, built in 1925, was to be the prototype of the future 'U1' class. This rebuild had in fact, been foreseen by Holcroft back in 1922, when the first production batch of tanks was authorised. He had suggested that, due to the range limitation already apparent, this batch be built as 2-6-0 tender types, and had, in fact, prepared some drawings. Clayton had been approached, but was not persuaded to take the matter up with Maunsell, who had shown a wish to pursue the tank design further.

One further outcome of the Sevenoaks incident was the vast improvement in the Southern permanent way as a result of the findings contained in the Ministry of Transport inquiry report, as follows:

> My examination, however, of the down track in the vicinity of the scene of this accident, and the actual survey made of the gauge and level of the rails, leads me to conclude that there was an insufficiency of hard and clean ballast foundation, a lack of proper drainage, and irregularities in the level and gauge of the rails, sufficient to set up serious rolling and lateral motion on tank engines travelling at high speeds. I cannot help believing that the heavy rainfall in the morning of the accident may have caused the track to go down rapidly under traffic, and have occasioned some of the irregularities subsequently observed and measured.

It is also perhaps worth mentioning that, even though he had come to the Southern from the SE&CR, Ellson's relationship with Maunsell was often strained, and the combination of the crash coming so soon after his promotion to the post of Chief Civil Engineer led to his suffering a nervous breakdown. As a result of this particular incident he also had a continual dislike of the employment of pony trucks on locomotives likely to be used for passenger traffic which was reflected in some future design studies, as we shall see in later chapters.

As a result of the criticism levelled at the railway in the accident report, reballasting took place using top quality rock ballast from Meldon quarry, and within two years the deficiencies were eliminated, by which time the whole class of 'River' tanks was no more. Never again did tank engines with pony trucks form the motive power for expresses on the Southern metals.

As a matter of interest, Gresley on the LNER had noticed the initial success of the 'K' class tanks on fast passenger services and, in 1925-26, drew up plans for a 2-6-4T for similar duties on that line. This design had 6 ft 2 in. coupled wheels, two 20 in. by 26 in. cylinders and a 'J39' boiler but, following the Sevenoaks accident and the adverse publicity given to fast tank locomotives, the design was dropped and the order for 10 examples transferred to Beyer, Peacock for a similar number of 'B12' 4-6-0s.

Even though Maunsell had, at this time, produced the 'K1' three-cylinder tank it is interesting to note that Gresley chose two cylinders for his abortive design.

Concurrent to the 'River' class accident, Maunsell had actually asked Holcroft to outline a scheme for the conversion of the ex-LB&SCR Baltics to 4-6-0 tender

L.B. Billinton's 0-6-0T, class 'E2', a development of which was proposed as a standard Southern branch line type by Maunsell.   *J.M. Jarvis Collection*

The 'Z' class 0-8-0 tank developed for shunting duties.   *J.H.L. Adams*

types using 'King Arthur' boilers and tenders. However, when actually carried out in 1934-5 the original boilers were repaired and retained, as they were in such good condition. It is clear from this design study that Richard foresaw problems with express tank locomotives in the future. Train weights were increasing and the limits imposed on non-stop range by the increased water consumption was threatening their continued use. Coupled with this was the sure knowledge that the Brighton line, on which the Baltics were almost exclusively employed, was a ripe candidate for electrification. This latter eventuality would mean displacing them onto longer routes where their range limitation would prove awkward, restricting their usefulness.

Maunsell was not finished with tank locomotives after the Sevenoaks disaster, but it is notable that all future designs were expressly for duties not involving passenger work. In late 1927 he ordered that some studies be initiated into the provision of a new 0-6-0T, to replace the large number of pre-Grouping designs. The ex-LB&SCR 'E2' class was the starting point. These tanks were primarily for shunting duties across the Southern and a total of 105 envisaged, but financial constraints resulted in cancellation of this design. The next tank to appear in traffic was the 'Z' class 0-8-0T, in 1929. Built for heavy shunting work on the Eastern and Central sections of the Southern, supplanting the existing Urie 'G16' class 4-8-0 tanks as well as replacing some of the elderly 0-6-0T types, the 'Z' employed some unique features. Firstly, due to experience on the type of work they were to be used for, in that a lot of time on shunting work is spent standing, the employment of a superheater was thought to be wasteful, as was the provision of a large grate area, demands for steam being intermittent. There had been an outstanding order for more of the 'G16' tanks which was cancelled and replaced by the 'Z' order for eight.

They were constructed in 1929 at Brighton, and were the last heavy duty shunting steam locomotives to be built by the Southern. Three cylinders were employed, primarily to ensure as even a torque as possible. The boiler was a standard Brighton design as used on the 'C3' 0-6-0 of 1906 vintage, and initially, conjugated valve motion was proposed. This was discontinued when it was found to produce an excessive overhang at the front end which could have been awkward in the close confines of a shunting yard. Accordingly, three sets of Walschaerts' gear were provided, with that for the middle cylinder employing a second eccentric utilised to give the movement usually obtained by the combination lever. The outside cylinders drove the third coupled axle, and the inside inclined cylinder drove the second axle. To cater for the tight curves often to be found in shunting yards the 4 ft 8 in. diameter wheels had side-play allowed on the leading and trailing axles. The locomotive was steam braked and vacuum braking was available if required. Water capacity was limited to 1,500 gallons, due to the small cut-away tanks, which improved the crew's visibility in the tight shunting confines of crowded yards.

Given the nickname 'Maggies' by the railwaymen, they all entered BR stock, being withdrawn in 1962 as a class, having been employed on their allotted task for the vast majority of their lives. There was one brief interlude in 1931 when an experiment was made to employ the 'Z' class on the Folkestone Harbour branch. The primary purpose was to see if an engine of this capacity, and based

One of the long-lasting 'R1' 0-6-0 tanks which were used for the duties at Folkestone harbour, refusing to be displaced by the 'Z'.   *Real Photographs*

The last of the 1932 batch of 'W' class tanks No. 1915 in immaculate lined black livery as the initial versions were when first turned out.   *MLS Collection*

on the 'Z', would be satisfactory. However, this proved unsuccessful due probably to the limited steaming capabilities endemic to the design. The high demand required on the steep gradient on this branch was at the limit which the combination of small firebox and large boiler could maintain for more than a very short time. To crown the episode, it had proved necessary to provide a new, stronger, swing bridge which provided access to the Harbour station to cater for the 71 ton locomotive. In the event, this was an inconclusive exercise and the ageing Stirling 'R1' 0-6-0Ts continued their reign until, in BR days, they were eventually replaced by some Pannier tanks drafted in from the Western Region.

The 'Z' tanks, with their specialised role of heavy duty shunting, were, despite their short wheelbase and associated front and rear overhang, functional and not ungainly looking engines. Clearly 'Maunsell' in conception, as shown by their Ashford cabs and distinctively sloped outside cylinder casings and deep front buffer beams which typified all of his early three-cylinder types. Their main advantage in service came from the three-cylinder layout which gave a more even torque and softer exhaust, this latter of considerable pleasure to those living in the vicinity of the yards employing them, due to the reduction in noise level. A further 10 were authorised in 1931 from Eastleigh, but cancelled due to the economic depression affecting the country at that time. By the time financial constraints had been lifted, the reinstatement of this order had been made unnecessary by the exercise to consider diesel-electric locomotives for shunting duties.

Despite the failure of the 2-6-4T 'River' class, Maunsell did design a further tank of this wheel arrangement, the 'W' class of 1931. These locomotives bore a strong resemblance to the three-cylinder version of the earlier 2-6-4T, and in fact used many of the parts removed during the rebuilding of the two cylinder variants, namely the side tanks and pony and bogie assemblies. They were closely related to the 'N1' class 2-6-0, having the same boiler, cylinders, motion and 5 ft 6 in. diameter driving wheels as these engines. A total of 15 was built, the initial five at Eastleigh in 1932, with the balance of 10 coming from Ashford in 1935-6. From the outset, they were prohibited from passenger use. Their main purpose was for cross-London freight traffic, which by 1930 was in desperate need of a powerful and modern locomotive. Versatile machines, they lasted well into BR days, being withdrawn for scrapping in 1963-4.

In 1936, Richard still pursued the needs for tank engines on the semi-fast passenger duties and branch line work in the design of a 2-6-2T, of which 20 were authorised in the early summer, but this order was cancelled in October. So the opportunity to begin updating the tank engine stock died, and had to wait until British Railways, when the BR Standard 2-6-2T made its appearance on Southern Region metals.

And thus ended Maunsell's design episodes involving tank locomotives. So far as aesthetics go, the 'River' and 'W' classes were graceful, well-proportioned engines, fully capable of accomplishing the tasks for which they were provided. The Sevenoaks accident blotted the copy-book of what otherwise would have been a successful continuation of the employment of tank engines on short-range high-speed express passenger services, so long as train weights were at the level current at that time. As time progressed and the weights increased beyond 300-350 tons, the tanks would have been approaching the limit of their range potential largely by the higher water consumption caused by increasing loads. So, in retrospect, it was perhaps fortuitous that the rebuilding of the 'Rivers' as tender locomotives took place when it did - it could well have been dictated by circumstances at not too much later a date. In fact, we have already seen that a further order for 30 tanks had already been altered to tender types (class 'U') before this accident forced a complete retraction from the policy of employing tank locomotives on express duties on the Eastern Section. Ellson retained almost a paranoic dislike of pony trucks on tank engines for the rest of his career, which continued once he was fully recovered from his breakdown.

Sometimes the 'W' class strayed out of their area, here No. 1912 is seen leaving Ashford on the 12.40 pm down Dover goods in 1938. Note the tower of Ashford Parish Church to the right of the signal box. Has the small boy in the foreground got stuck?

D.B. Barnard

Chapter Nine

Electrification and Other Issues

It is difficult to know where to place the other major issues involving the attention of Maunsell, in particular those connected with the Southern's electrification programme, which as CME he had responsibility for in terms of integration and stock throughout his time in that position. The SE&CR had, after the end of the War, commenced planning for widespread electrification of all its London area network. This would eventually have been extended onto the main lines for the longer runs. It was a complex scheme, employing multiple units for the suburban runs and electric locomotives for the longer distance passenger and freight services. Maunsell would have been intimately involved with the discussions involving this modernisation plan. Like the LSWR system the SE&CR proposed using third rail current collection, but with a protected live rail to pass the 1,500 volts DC specified. No physical work had been started, mainly due to the blockage of the railway's intention to build its own power station at Angerstein Wharf on the Thames. This blockage emanated from the Electricity Commissioners and the Ministry of Transport, as not being in line with the current government policy of using already available sources of energy. The LSWR, having commenced its electrification in 1915, had not had this restriction placed on them at that time, and provided the current required from its own power station at Durnsford Road, Wimbledon, via a series of substations at intervals along the lines.

But to return to the Southern, the phasing in of electric suburban services was a task which definitely caused some headaches in the early days in respect of the Locomotive Replenishment Fund. Up to 1931, we know from Sir Herbert Walker's own statement, that some £11.8 million had been spent to electrify some 293 route-miles (or 800 track-miles) of the complex suburban network in the Southern territory. Almost half this expenditure had been charged to the capital account. It was to lead directly to the limitation to 16 locomotives when the 'Lord Nelson' class was constructed. Sixteen was really insufficient to permit these locomotives to be used to the maximum effect on all the services for which they were planned, particularly when it is realised that some two or three would be unavailable due to the routine maintenance and, eventually, overhauls. A fuller analysis of this limitation will be found in Chapter Eleven. Perhaps here is an example of Richard Maunsell not coming to grips with the need to make a cast-iron case for new locomotives to the accountants who had the ultimate say in the allocation of capital funds. Sir Herbert Walker was a passionate believer in the electrification programme and it appears his tremendous personality held such sway that even Maunsell was unable to provide more convincing arguments. As a result, the 'Lord Nelson' episode indicated a reticence, or inability, to press the accountants for adequate funding that a larger fleet would entail. More such locomotives would have permitted better, more economical, use to be made of them over a wider area. For, despite the criticisms levelled at them, the 'Nelsons', handled correctly, were first-class

'T9' class 4-4-0 No. 337 as rebuilt by Maunsell with superheater.   *Real Photographs*

Drummond class 'D15' No. 466 at Eastleigh in 1931.   *Real Photographs*

engines, even drawing praise from Oliver Bulleid for their capabilities and wide route availability.

One of Maunsell's first jobs on taking office at Waterloo, had been to order a detailed evaluation of the Southern's steam motive power situation. This produced the not surprising fact that a surplus of medium powered locomotives would arise in the near future as a result of the expansion of the electrification. A series of trials were instigated to determine which classes could be scrapped at next major overhaul and which could be retained for secondary duties. The results of these trials were never published outside the Southern and the summary of results was only unearthed at Ashford in 1957 during a drawing office clear-out. The outcome of these tests ensured the retention of the ex-LSWR Drummond class 'T9' until early BR days, and the quick demise of many of the ex-LB&SCR types involved.

Maunsell worked with Alfred Raworth, the engineer for New Works, in the provision of stock for the electrification improvements, and by converting some of the existing steam suburban compartment coaches, considerable economies were achieved. Even the old four and six-wheel coaches were used, in that their bodies were combined on new bogie underframes. Herbert Jones, the chief electrical engineer, was responsible for the installation of the 600 volt third-rail system chosen, together with the necessary power supply and sub-stations to feed this to the track at regular intervals.

Maunsell, Raworth and Jones had, it is recorded, a harmonious working relationship, which speaks volumes for the former's executive abilities, as the latter two were asking for the injection of large capital sums which necessarily restricted that available for new locomotives. But a CME's job is not only to provide more locomotives, it covers the whole spectrum of engineering work connected with motive power and stock needs of a railway, so involvement in the electrification programme was *de rigueur*. Also, political diversions raised their head shortly after Grouping in the form of the General Strike in 1926. This eventually caused some shortages in coal supplies and so recourse to oil-burning for some of the locomotives was commenced. Maunsell dispatched Holcroft to Derby on 26th May carrying a personal request for assistance to his old colleague of Horwich days, Sir Henry Fowler. Apparently, Clayton was a bit nettled at this, as he had always considered liaison with Derby his preserve. However, Holcroft was then sent to Eastleigh to oversee the fitting of the Derby oil-firing system to selected locomotives. It is on record that the capital cost per engine for this installation was £110, and it took 48 hours to fit and just 8 hours to dismantle and return the engine to its coal-burning standard. A Drummond 'D15' No. E470, was the first fitted. The swift conclusion of the strike rendered many more conversions unnecessary, but it was felt that the experience gained would be useful in later years if a repetition of any coal shortage appeared.

By 1929, Walker had made his famous announcement to the Traffic Officers' Conference: 'Gentlemen, I have decided to electrify to Brighton'. This meant a requirement for multiple units of a different format to those employed on the suburban services, as corridors, gangways between coaches, lavatories and catering vehicles were all needed to permit an equivalent level of comfort to the steam stock for the passengers. The operating characteristics were to be similar to the existing suburban units.

'4-COR' No. 3056 is seen heading a Waterloo-Portsmouth service in June 1937.

British Railways

Maunsell had established his own brand of solid wood and steel steam stock, which was used for the basis of his early multiple units for the Brighton electrification. For some time, in fact, since the introduction of the new SE&CR Continental boat train stock in 1921, Richard had specified the buck-eye coupler for sets of steam stock (but electric stock never had buck-eye couplers in Southern days), a feature which would certainly have been logical on the electrics as they were made up of a fixed rake of vehicles, only uncoupled for maintenance purposes. Many of the fixed rakes of steam stock were so fitted, but the individual coaches used for making up particular trains were left with either conventional couplings or combined buckeye and normal drawgear to permit lengthening or dividing of trains at will, on the longer runs where multiple destinations were served by one service. This latter was a feature of Southern operations to, in particular, the West Country holiday resorts.

The final episode of electrification involving Richard Maunsell was the initiation of design of stock for the Portsmouth (via Guildford) run, which was opened in mid-1937. The four-car units that resulted employed end gangways so that it was possible to pass from one set to another - the earlier Brighton six-car sets not having this facility. These particular sets were quickly dubbed 'Nelsons' due to firstly, their ultimate destination and, secondly, the one-eyed appearance given by the single off-set driver's window. The 5.04 pm from Victoria for Portsmouth Harbour via Sutton, Dorking and Horsham, which figured in the author's college days, was invariably made up of three sets of this stock, the centre one having a Buffet car. If finances ran to it, my one excess was to indulge in a cup of BR tea *en route* home, the trick being to drink it unspilled, such was the rough-riding of this stock.

All these electrification issues were, obviously, intertwined with large reorganisations of the carriage, wagon and locomotive works facilities inherited from the three railways which were merged to form the Southern. Recognising these problems and the need to reorganise matters so that the strong points of the best works could take the loads from the less efficient ones, Maunsell accordingly set about to rationalise the whole manufacturing and repair facilities to serve the Southern in the future.

The oldest works were at Ashford, dating from 1849, and had grown in rather piecemeal fashion. This plant was also geared towards the smaller type of engine, as this had been the policy of the SE&CR. Maunsell had found, on his arrival in 1913, that the works was not operating at its peak potential, with too much priority given to repairs, and had instigated a complete reorganisation, under Pearson, to permit more new builds to emanate from there. But he still had to turn to outside contractors in the pre-Grouping days in order to ensure that the required locomotives appeared on time. One further important addition to the facilities at Ashford in 1924 was the establishment of a Physical Laboratory. This department worked closely with the Materials Inspection Office and was also used to conduct research work in connection with equipment and suppliers. With routine testing of failure causes, Maunsell had at his command a modern technical department offering answers to improved reliability of locomotives and stock. Also installed in 1924 was the first electro-plating plant to be used on the Southern.

Eastleigh Locomotive Works as laid out by Robert Urie.

Author

Eastleigh, in terms of age, was the youngest of the facilities, the locomotive works having been constructed in 1910. As a result it was the best laid out and, in fact was to be the major production centre over Maunsell's and Bulleid's reigns. However, the machinery was a bit dated and required replacing with something more modern. This latter feature being dealt with, Maunsell then set about consolidating Eastleigh as the primary plant for new construction by injecting some of his SE&CR developed design philosophy. He accordingly transferred some of the junior draughtsmen from Ashford to work under T.S. Finlayson, the Chief Draughtsman at Eastleigh, whilst putting the works under the control of a fellow Irishman, Eyre Turbett. Turbett had trained at Crewe and, during the War, had worked with Maunsell on Government matters at Richborough. These examples are typical of Richard's grasp of the situation as regards the embodiment of his own brand of ideas in an organisation built up and nurtured under Robert Urie. He had his own plans on Southern locomotive development and wished to see them infused into the design offices and production facilities at Eastleigh.

The third works, Brighton, was intended to be run down to a care and maintenance basis before eventual closure. Brighton works had been built in 1852, on a site which prevented effective expansion without creating difficulties in transfer between shops, due to its multi-level aspect.

On the carriage side of things, Ashford carriage works was particularly inefficient, with part of the works only able to cope with the now obsolete four- and six-wheel stock. All new carriage construction was therefore placed at Eastleigh and the maintenance switched to Lancing, the former LB&SCR carriage works, which Richard placed in the capable hands of G.H. Gardener. Both these plants were capable of flow-line production, the latter eventually achieving an overhaul throughput of no less than 2,500 vehicles per year, thanks to the expertise of Gardener, who expanded the workforce by having the necessary personnel transferred from other works. Carriage design was left in the capable hands of Surrey Warner at Eastleigh, who had developed the LSWR 'Ironclad' form of corridor stock for that railway just prior to Grouping. It was this particular design that was chosen by Maunsell to be used as the basis for his standard Southern stock.

Once the carriage, wagon and locomotive works situation had been resolved Maunsell turned his attention to the working practices for locomotive overhaul. Up to now (about 1928-9) it had been the accepted norm that one gang would carry out the complete overhaul of a locomotive, moving with it through the shops. The revised policy was to set up specialist groups of workers who remained in one place, the engine being moved in stages through their hands. This change had a dramatic effect on the time it took to carry out a general repair, which in the case of 'King Arthur', dropped from three months to just 19 or 20 days. The cost savings were considerable, at a time when such matters were of prime importance in a country struggling through a time of recession.

These reorganisations, both of works and working practices, were to benefit the Southern for the rest of its days, particularly during the War years to come, and stemmed from a 1927 visit to the Crewe works of the LMS which came about as follows. Between 1925-27 the works at Crewe was reorganised and

Brighton locomotive works, as reconstituted after Maunsell retired, in preparation for the forthcoming War.

Author

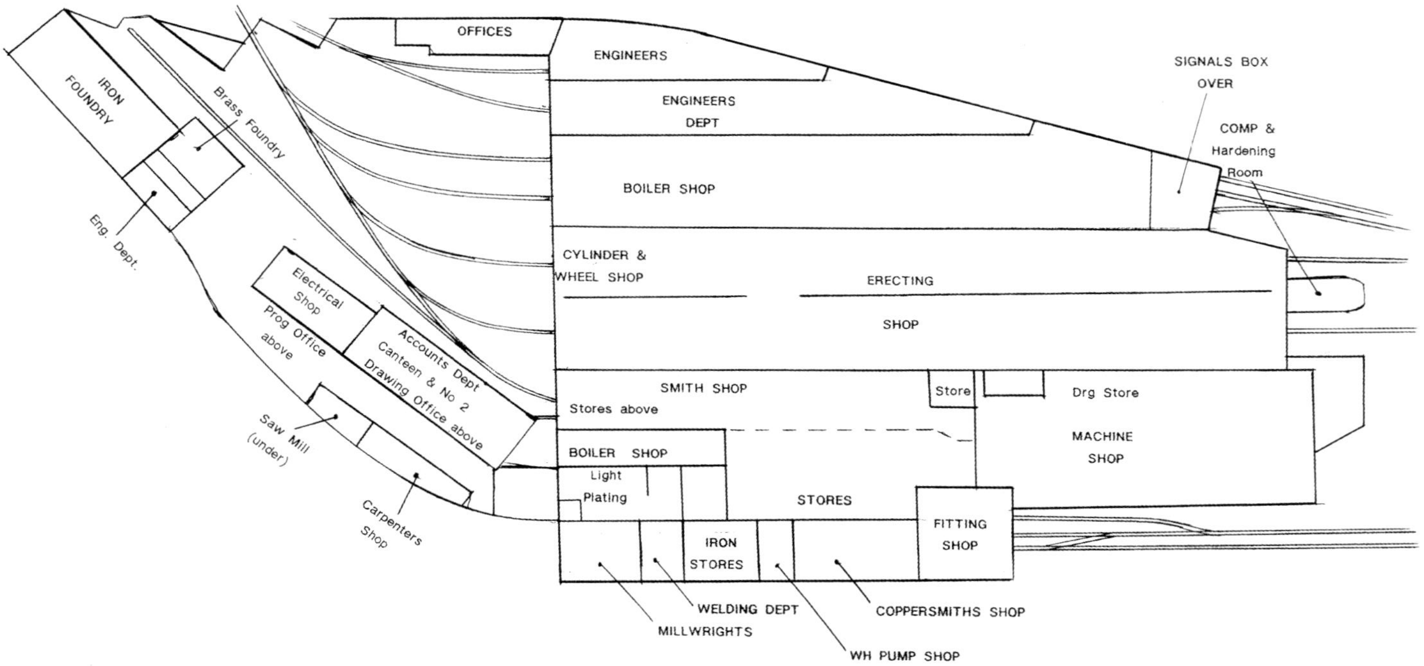

Plan labels:

SIGNALS BOX OVER

COMP & Hardening Room

Drg Store

MACHINE SHOP

Store

FITTING SHOP

COPPERSMITHS SHOP

WH PUMP SHOP

STORES

ERECTING SHOP

WELDING DEPT

MILLWRIGHTS

IRON STORES

ENGINEERS

ENGINEERS DEPT

BOILER SHOP

CYLINDER & WHEEL SHOP

SMITH SHOP

Stores above

BOILER SHOP

Light Plating

OFFICES

Brass Foundry

Electrical Shop

Prog Office above

Accounts Dept

Canteen & No 2 Drawing Office above

Carpenters Shop

Saw Mill (under)

IRON FOUNDRY

Eng. Dept.

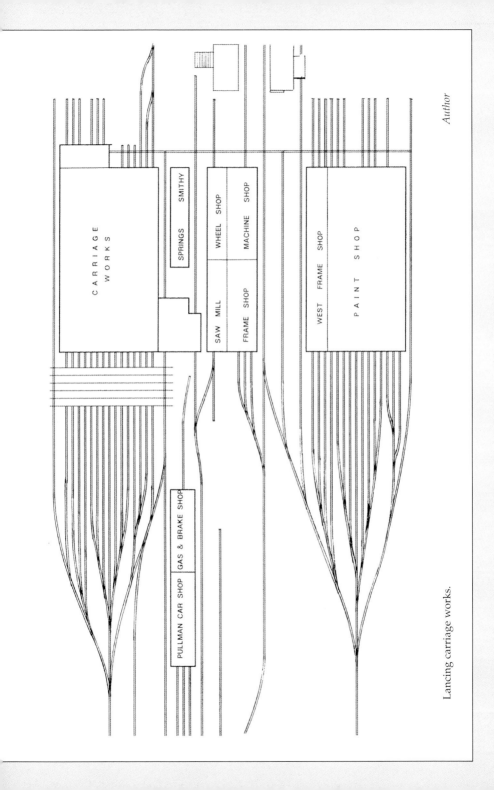

Lancing carriage works.

rebuilt to bring modern flow-line practices into the locomotive building and repair areas. Sir Henry Fowler, the then CME, was justly proud of the results this produced, although it had actually been planned and instigated by his predecessor, George Hughes. When it was substantially complete the other CME's were invited to view the results. The 27th May, 1927 found Richard Maunsell and Nigel Gresley at Crewe being conducted around by Sir Henry. The potential of flow-line techniques was noted by Maunsell and eventually adopted on the Southern at Eastleigh, as we have seen.

When the Southern was formed, one of the many items to be discussed at Board level and coming within the remit of the CME was that of the choice of livery for locomotives and passenger rolling stock. Early in 1924, five coaches were lined up at Ashford for inspection by the Directors. Richard's own choice was a dark blue lined out in white, yellow and red. Also on display was brown with yellow lining and gold lettering, the standard LSWR green, LB&SCR umber and the SE&CR chestnut. Out of those on display they chose the green used by the LSWR as the one to be applied. The LSWR had used two shades of green originally, a sage green for locomotives adopted by Robert Urie and a darker 'Parsons Green' for coaches, including those of the electric stock. Maunsell used up the existing stocks of these colours until 1925, when the darker coach colour was applied to locomotives as well. This remained the standard until the final year of his regime.

There is a fascinating tale concerning a discussion on liveries which apparently took place in 1936 when Maunsell, E.S. Cox and Frank Bushrod visited the Isle of Wight. Sir Herbert Walker was also present, but remained outside the arguments that ensued. The original purpose of this visit was probably an inspection tour, and on the way to Portsmouth a conversation started on the effect of rolling stock livery on passenger bookings. So far as locomotives were concerned, Cox and Bushrod plumped for green, the former also specifying gold lining. Richard stated his preference for dark unlined grey with large white numbers - a throwback to his earlier days on the SE&CR when he had introduced this livery in place of the intricate lined-out green of Wainwright. Sir Herbert obviously had listened to all that was said, for later on that day he produced a length of green cord, cut it into four lengths and distributed it to the others with the statement: 'That will be the colour Southern engines and coaches shall be painted in future'. Some authorities attribute the Malachite green to this episode, but this colour did not materialise until towards the end of 1938, when Bulleid was established as CME. There was a brief time in late 1937 and early 1938 when an experimental livery of light olive green appeared on some stock and it is generally presumed that this is the one chosen by Walker.

As regards Maunsell's approach to the training of future engineers on the Southern, and indeed on the SE&CR previously, it may be appropriate here to survey how his interests in their progress took an important place in his CME's responsibilities. Nutured by his own pupilage with Ivatt and Aspinall, Richard always made time for his pupils and premium apprentices. He was permitted five pupils plus 15 premium apprentices (five each at Ashford, Brighton and Eastleigh). The pupilage lasted a minimum of three years and the fee charged was £150 per year. So far as the premium apprentices were concerned the annual fee was £60 over the five years of their apprenticeship. These fees were, as usual, part of the CME's 'perks'.

The interest Maunsell took in his pupils and apprentices is borne out in the following examples.

Henry Dannatt, a pupil from 1936-38, writes:

> When at Ashford in the winters of 1936 and 37 Mr Maunsell would see me every Saturday morning in his office at Ashford works. He would ask me what shops I was spending my time in and took an active interest in what I had to say. He would also ask the Shop Foreman from time to time to ensure that I was getting experience in all matters.

Douglas Barnard, who was a premium apprentice at Ashford from 1934-9, writes:

> I was interviewed by Maunsell sometime in 1935 while still in the fitting shop. He had been asked to see me by Percy Wainwright, a friend of my family, who was a brother of H.S. Wainwright (CME of the SE&CR prior to Maunsell), and who had himself been apprenticed at Ashford in his youth, but had been an Inspecting Engineer and latterly with a firm called Turton, Platt & Co. In 1935 he was retired and lived at Herne Bay.
>
> Although I may not have realised it at the time, it now seems that in my apprenticeship I gained greater experience at the works as a result of this meeting with Maunsell by going where others did not get, i.e. experience in the Physical Laboratory, with an introduction to the testing of materials and actual inspecting, also I did a period on the marking off table which others did not get. Two apprentices each year were also given 6 months running shed experience, including 3 months on the footplate, and then 6 months in the drawing office, all of which I obtained, finishing my apprenticeship on 3rd September, 1939, the day World War II began.

We can see in this latter extract the parallels between Richard's own experiences on the L&YR under Aspinall in 1892, particularly the running shed assignment. Both Henry Dannatt and Douglas Barnard were involved in the Pupil and Premium Apprentice Association (PPAA) at Ashford, an organisation actively encouraged by Maunsell. This association had started in the early 1920s and had branches at all the Southern works. In 1926 the first annual dinner was held at the South Western Hotel in Southampton, at which Maunsell was the principal guest and, to the Eastleigh contingent, in a social context, an unknown quantity. However, Richard appeared to enjoy himself and, following the Chairman's proposal of a toast to the CME there was a rendering of the rather ebullient PPAA song:

> We are old Maunsell's army, what b . . . . . good are we?
> We cannot work, we cannot play, or say our ABC.
> But when we get to Waterloo, old Maunsell he will say,
> Hoch! Hoch! Mein Gott, what a b . . . . . fine lot,
> Are the boys of the PPAA.

Maunsell rose to speak and the company waited with baited breath following their somewhat impertinent rendering. He smiled, and then broke into hearty

The photograph Maunsell had taken for his pupils and premium apprentices in 1937, shortly before he retired.
H.M. Dannatt

laughter, before launching into a speech full of Irish humour and finished with a typical blunt statement:

> Now I am going to promise you people something. If any of you get into trouble in the works, or are not getting on as you would like, or are worried about anything, you can always ask to see me personally and I will see what I can do to put things right. But, I warn you, if anyone comes to me with a childish or trivial complaint, he will leave my office a sorrier and wiser man.

The PPAA continued for many years and was only to fade out with the onset of World War II. Douglas Barnard writes:

> Their main function was to arrange outings to other works such as Crewe, Swindon, Doncaster, etc. which usually took place on a Saturday. Sometimes we were allowed free travel for these, otherwise we went at Privilege Ticket rate. An annual dinner was held at the Charing Cross Hotel to which 'high-ups' would be invited, Maunsell, Pearson, Holcroft, Hicks, J.T. Finch (Progress Office), Joe Palmer (Chief Draughtsman), Clayton, etc. The dinner would include the singing by the apprentices of the PPAA song to the tune of 'From Greenland's Icy Mountains'.

In these later years, close to his retirement, Maunsell was unable to attend these dinners, as his increasing ill-health affected him. Usually, Clayton or one of the others mentioned above was present and would deliver an encouraging speech to those assembled.

Another function at which Richard presided, so long as his health permitted, was the annual Technical Staff dinner held at the Charing Cross Hotel. The social interchange at this function ensured that those who saw Maunsell infrequently were able to meet and converse with their CME in an informal atmosphere.

Before we look at the express locomotive developments of Maunsell, a short diversion onto the railbus story is appropriate. There had been some limited tests with a 22-seat railbus in the mid-1920s, which had shown promise, and so, armed with the results of these tests and a proposal from the Sentinel Company, Maunsell asked for, and got, funds to purchase a prototype model of a 44-passenger steam-powered railbus. Holcroft was given the responsibility of overseeing this exercise and, in March 1933, proceeded up to the Metropolitan Cammell works at Birmingham where the vehicle was ready for delivery. After some minor modifications to the brakes, it was driven from Birmingham to Brighton via Willesden and the West London line. It was located at Brighton so that the bus could be evaluated on the Devils Dyke branch. For two years, with the minimum of problems, the Sentinel railbus served this branch, and Maunsell was sufficiently impressed to ask for a quote for five more vehicles to be used on other lightly-used branches of the Southern. The quote that came back was much in excess of that anticipated, and so the expansion was cancelled and eventually died when the single example went in for major repairs and overhaul. The original quote for the initial example had, obviously, been aimed low in the hope that it would be a foregone conclusion that a follow-up order would materialise. Metropolitan Cammell clearly misjudged Richard's straight

A rare shot of the railbus in action on the Dyke branch date unknown, but around 1933-4, as this was the time it was used on the Dyke run.   *MLS Collection*

dealing reputation and the company missed the opportunity of a substantial order. However, further orders beyond this would most certainly have been limited by the advent, in the mid-1930s, of the diesel railbus.

One further responsibility, in which any CME was now to be found involved, lay with the motor transport vehicles which played an increasingly important part of a railway's infrastructure for the delivery of goods from the station yards. Maunsell accordingly set about the establishment of repair shops at strategic locations which were to deal with the various types of motor vehicles thus employed, which grew in number from just 140 at Grouping to 736 by 1938.

Chapter Ten

Carriage Stock Developments
on the Southern

At this point it is appropriate to take a brief look at the carriage side of things in greater detail and see how Maunsell dealt with matters. So often the provision of passenger stock and goods stock is glossed over when considering the achievements of a CME, but a railway must continually be aware of the need to attract passengers and provide suitably attractive and comfortable carriages. The important task of deciding just how this was to be achieved within a reasonable cost and time fell ultimately on the shoulders of the CME and his executive staff.

Prior to Grouping, the carriage stock of the three constituent railways that made up the Southern was in a rather poor state. Only the LSWR and, to a limited extent, the SE&CR had new modern corridor stock in existence or being built. Excursion stock was particularly bad, six-wheelers had been commonplace before the War and those still existing were worn out from heavy use on troop specials.

One of the developments in the industrial scene which emerged as a result of the improvements in the workplace over the 1920s was the advent of paid holidays. This meant that many more people would be taking holidays away and, the main mode of travel to the resorts would be by train.

The Southern provided a large number of holiday routes to South Coast resorts and, as a result, the need to provide adequate carriage stock was pressing at the time Maunsell took office at Grouping. Whilst continuing to see existing carriage orders placed prior to Grouping were fulfilled, his main priority was to decide which of the existing designs could be used for the development of a standard Southern design. The main thrust was to be for the corridor stock, as the commuter and short-haul stock situation was being adequately covered by the continuous rebuilding of some of the existing stock into electric units plus, of course, the provision of the new 'Bull Nose' units as the electrification programme spread into and beyond the suburbs. There were also adequate surplus compartment stock sets displaced from the electrification area to cope with requirements elsewhere as the obsolescent stock of that type was progressively scrapped.

The advent of the War meant that any meaningful carriage stock developments on the SE&CR had to be put on one side. Although Wainwright had been primarily a carriage man, his preoccupation with the locomotive side of things before Maunsell took office, meant that new carriage developments had been minimal. Hence, one of Maunsell's priorities after the War ended, and the Continental boat trains were reinstated, was to have Lionel Lynes design and produce an 8-coach corridor train for the Victoria to Dover Marine services. These new coaches, with a body length of 62 ft and width of 8 ft, were put into service in August 1921 and were the prototypes for what became known as the 'Continental' corridor stock. Some unusual features of these designs were that the brake coaches were not gangwayed at the outer ends, which had standard

Corridor Brake Composite No. 6575 as preserved on the Bluebell Railway 27th April, 1997.

Author

Open Third No. 1309 as preserved on Bluebell Railway 27th April, 1997. A most elegant design.

Author

screw couplings and buffers; the rest of the rake had Pullman gangways and buckeye couplers. The Pullman gangways were standard as frequently one or more Pullman cars would be marshalled into the train. The end entry doors originally opened inwards, though in later years these were changed to outward opening, and the sides had the lower panels neatly matchboarded.

This design proved successful, for a further 67 examples (41 of which were built by outside contractors) to be ordered before and after Grouping, there being insufficient time to wait for a standard Southern design to be formulated, such was the demand for increased boat train services.

With the boat train stock situation under control, in the early days of the Southern Maunsell and Lynes proceeded to design more corridor stock for the former SE&CR routes to the Kent coast resorts. These coaches embodied many South Eastern features and had a body length of 57 ft and width of 8 ft 6 in. and in many ways could be construed as the precursors of the future standard Maunsell stock. However, this was to be more akin to the LSWR 'Ironclad' design, as we shall see later. Some 77 examples were built of Composite, Third and Third Brake types to make up nine 8-coach sets. Eastleigh produced five sets and Lancing four sets, delivery being completed by May 1925. The title 'Thanet' stock was given to these examples. It was this type of stock which made up the train involved in the Sevenoaks crash in 1927.

Turning now to the origin of what became known as the Maunsell standard stock, just prior to Grouping, Eastleigh had commenced production of Surrey Warner's 'Ironclad' stock. These acquired their name from the fact that the wooden bodies were clad in steel sheet, and were instantly recognisable by their outside-framed 9 ft wheelbase bogies.

Never one to make a decision without first weighing up the situation, Richard discussed carriage matters with those intimately concerned. As a result it was not until the 30th April, 1924 meeting of the Locomotive, Carriage and Electrical Committee that he tabled the authorisation of a further batch of 'Ironclad' stock to be used on the Waterloo-Bournemouth, Swanage and Lymington and also the London Bridge-Brighton services. The latter service coaches were in fact constructed at Lancing, the last to be built there prior to the switch of that works to a purely maintenance role.

Production of the 'Ironclad' coaches in their original form ceased in late 1925. The first design change was incorporated in the final batch, being the change of the bogies to 8 ft wheelbase single-bolster type, which was to remain standard for some time.

By this time, the designs for a range of standard corridor stock had been completed at Eastleigh, and in April 1925 Maunsell requested the Rolling Stock Committee to authorise the construction of 72 examples. The body design and construction was a slightly lengthened version of the 'Ironclads', with the underframes and bogies showing considerable Ashford influence stemming from the 'Thanet' stock exercise. These designs soon became known as 'Maunsell' stock and continued being built for the remainder of his days on the Southern. One major styling change appearing around 1929, this being the incorporation of high windows in the corridors, presumably due to standing passengers complaining they had to stoop in order to see out easily, so it has been suggested.

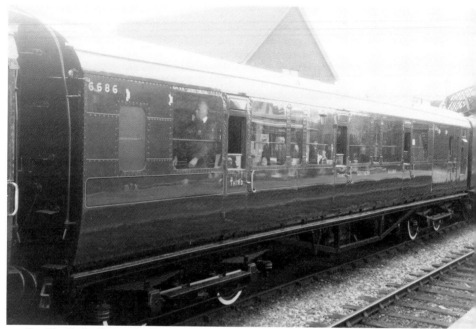

Corridor Brake Composite No. 6686 as preserved on the Bluebell Railway 27th April, 1997. The differences between this and No. 6575 are purely internal. This illustrates the coach from the corridor side.   *Author*

An ex-SE&CR 10-compartment Third, built at Ashford in the early days of Maunsell's tenure with the aim of future conversion to electric stock, but not in fact done.   *Author*

Perhaps uniquely, Maunsell carriage stock was to be found in three body widths, 9 ft, 8 ft 6 in. and 8 ft. The first was for the Western and Central Sections, the second for the Eastern Section and the third exclusively for the Hastings line with its restricted tunnel widths.

As the 1930s approached, the private car became more accessible and the railways sensed competition looming. The spectre of the car, with its immediacy and flexibility, becoming the means of transport to holiday resorts, drove the railway companies to counter the threat by offering major improvements in passenger comfort. The Maunsell coaches were designed with such matters in the forefront, the absolute right of passenger preference was paramount. Adequate luggage space was always provided, based on a rule of thumb of three trunks per family, with some of the Brake Thirds having luggage compartments taking half the available volume. However, the other side of the coin dictated that high density, but comfortable, stock was needed to attract the ever larger numbers of potential passengers who were benefiting from the growing trend of paid holidays whilst not yet being in a position to afford a motor car. A large number of Open Thirds and 8-compartment Thirds were built and were seen to be marshalled with the more plush sets in many holiday trains. The Open Thirds were often to be found marshalled next to Restaurant/Kitchen cars, as they had provision for tables to be fitted between facing sets of seats which could provide extra restaurant capacity on the longer runs.

The South Coast resorts were easily accessible by road from the major industrial centres of the South-East, and the Southern coped well with the competition initially by the provision of the corridor and vestibule stock, plus a good advertising campaign. The electrification to Brighton and other coastal areas helped considerably by providing fast, clean connections with the new sets derived largely from the steam stock then in production. Maunsell thus had his coaches in the steam and electric areas over the whole of the Southern, and they formed a major part of the trains bringing in the all-important traffic receipts upon which the railway depended.

By 1933, some 1,065 new carriages for the steam-hauled services had been built. Surrey Warner had retired in 1929, his responsibilities being given to Lionel Lynes, who had faithfully served Maunsell from 1914. A further 396 carriages were to be built for steam-hauled use up to 1936, when orders ceased. The Southern was to build no more new steam carriage stock until 1945, and the existing stock levels were to carry it through the forthcoming War with remarkably few losses due to enemy action, just 16 to be precise. It remained for British Railways progressively to withdraw the 1,445 examples of Maunsell coaches they acquired.

Readers interested in the details of Maunsell's coaching stock can find this in *Bogie Carriages of the SE&CR* and *Maunsell's SR Steam Carriage Stock*, both written by David Gould and published by The Oakwood Press.

'Lord Nelson' class 4-6-0 No. 861 *Lord Anson* carrying the number and nameplates from No. 850 *Lord Nelson* at the Liverpool & Manchester Railway centenary celebrations in 1930

Chapter Eleven

A Four-Cylinder Adventure and the Masterpiece

Undoubtedly, the locomotives for which Maunsell was most famous were the 4-6-0 'Lord Nelson' and the 4-4-0 'Schools' classes, both evolved in the middle to late 1920s.

Whilst the latter were an almost immediate success, the former were beset by a few early problems which were never fully resolved during Maunsell's time in office. However, the 'Nelsons' did eventually prove useful and reliable engines when properly handled by the crews.

The Traffic Department of the Southern, in 1923, had stated the need for a locomotive to cope with 500 ton trains at an average start-to-stop speed of 55 mph, with the holiday services to the West Country specifically in mind. None of the existing stock was capable of meeting this demanding specification with complete confidence, so Maunsell was charged with designing a suitable type. By this time he had installed himself and his immediate team of personal assistants, James Clayton and Harold Holcroft, at Waterloo. Clayton and Holcroft were the two who influenced many of the designs attributable to Maunsell. Holcroft had, in 1920, put forward a proposal to set the cranks of a four-cylinder locomotive at 135 degrees to give a smooth torque when pulling hard and also, by virtue of a smoother blast, produce a more even flow of air through the firebed.

The immediate decision to be made was whether the new express type should be a 4-6-0 or 4-6-2? This was resolved by dispatching Clayton on some footplate trips, firstly on a GWR 'Castle' class from Paddington to Plymouth and, secondly, on an LNER Pacific from Kings Cross to Grantham. How much the number of cylinders played in this assessment has not come to light, but it is interesting that the four-cylinder 'Castle' won hands-down over the three-cylinder Pacific. And so the new type was to be a four-cylinder 4-6-0, and schemes began on this basis. This practical way in which Richard Maunsell approached the decision as to the wheel layout was typical of his natural caution when approaching what was to be a new design in all respects. After all, considerable investment was to be involved in the production of the resulting design, investment which was hard to justify without sound evidence of the practicality of the proposed locomotive.

As an interim measure, whilst the initial studies into the new, large, express type were under way, a further 15 'N15' 4-6-0s were ordered, to bolster up the continuing production of 'King Arthur' express locomotives, which eventually totalled some 74 in number. These 15 consisted of five rebuilds of Drummond 'F13s', the remaining 10 being new builds to the original Urie design.

Of these 'N15s', the order for the final batch of 15, placed with Eastleigh, was modified to 14 'King Arthurs' and one new 4-6-0 type, this latter being the prototype for what was to become the 'Lord Nelson' class.

The 135 degree crank feasibility was proved viable by rebuilding one of the Drummond 4-6-0s, No. 449, with this setting for testing. No problems were to

'Royal Scot' class 4-6-0 No. 6159 (un-named) on the up 'Irish Mail'.   *Real Photographs*

A particularly good action shot of 'Lord Nelson' class No. 863 *Lord Rodney* on a boat express. The coach in view is of the ex-SE&CR Continental stock.   *MLS Collection*

be found and the concept became a standard feature for the 'Nelson' design. By the end of 1925, the drawings were complete and construction at Eastleigh had commenced. So far as Eastleigh was concerned, both the Belpaire firebox and working pressure of 220 lb./sq. in. were departures from their previous practice. On 10th August, 1926, Richard accompanied the Directors on a visit to Eastleigh works to view the newly-constructed prototype, No. 850, as yet un-named and in works grey. After the initial running-in period, the engine was put on the Waterloo-Salisbury-Waterloo run of the 'Atlantic Coast Express', with Maunsell and representatives of the press on board. The up train was no less than 10 minutes late into Salisbury, but a fine effort by the 'Nelson' prototype regained no less than eight minutes on a splendid run up to Waterloo, which gave an immediate good impression to those on board.

The ultimate tractive effort of 33,500 lb. led to the claim, valid only for a short time,* by the Public Relations department of the Southern, that they had 'The Most Powerful Passenger Engine in Great Britain'.

Perhaps the greatest event in the early days of the 'Nelsons' was the derivation of the LMS 'Royal Scot' class from Maunsell's design. We have already covered the aspects surrounding one railway company supplying another with new locomotives in Chapter Four. The 'Royal Scot' story evolved thus. The LMS Chief Mechanical Engineer, Sir Henry Fowler, was given less than a year to provide 50 express locomotives for the summer traffic of 1927. The power needed was equivalent to that of the GWR 'Castle' class 4-6-0. The GWR refused point-blank even to supply a set of drawings when approached, so Fowler approached Maunsell, who was much more co-operative, and arranged for a set of 'Nelson' drawings to be supplied to the North British Locomotive Company, which was prepared to tender for this order and its extremely tight time schedule. The liaison between the Southern and the LMS was, so far as the latter were concerned, placed in the hands of Herbert Chambers, chief locomotive draughtsman at Derby. He went to Waterloo to talk with Maunsell, Clayton and Holcroft and later briefed the North British Locomotive Co. as to what was required of them.

The subsequent events are legendary in locomotive history, particularly when it is realised that the LMS Operating Department specified three cylinders and sundry other modifications to conform with their practices and standards. The locomotives were delivered only a few weeks behind the very optimistic schedule, and put into service immediately. They proved very successful from the outset, and it seems surprising that Maunsell did not instigate some liaison with the builders in view of the superior steaming of the 'Royal Scots' when compared to the 'Nelsons'.

However, to return to the Southern scene, the prototype 4-6-0, No. 850 was assigned to Nine Elms and on 27th September, 1927 entered passenger service to Bournemouth from Waterloo, before being switched to trials on the 'Atlantic Coast Express' as far as Salisbury. Following this introduction on the Western Section the engine was transferred to Battersea and given trials on the Dover boat trains until early December. During this lengthy running-in session, it was ordered to proceed to Ashford to be shown off to the Duke and Duchess of York who were visiting the Works. To Richard fell the duty of escorting the Royal

---

* This claim was displaced by the emergence of the GWR 'King' class 4-6-0 in 1927, with a tractive effort of 40,000 lb.

couple round the shops, to explain the purpose of the machinery and equipment. The Duke and Duchess were introduced to the foreman in charge of each shop during their tour and, finally, were conducted onto the footplate of the 'Lord Nelson', which was pulling the special train. The Duke, under the close supervision of driver Francis and Richard Maunsell, opened the regulator and drove the train into Ashford station. Following this brief assignment it returned to Nine Elms. Further testing involving a brief time at Salisbury, working to Exeter, then followed prior to a further return to Nine Elms.

The final test came on 10th April, 1927, when a special train of 16 coaches weighing 521 tons was run to Salisbury at the required average speed of 55 mph. The coal consumption associated with this heavy train was a staggering 66½ lb. per mile, almost double that achieved on the earlier trials with, admittedly, lighter loads. However, this consumption indicated that potential problems in steaming lay ahead, and which, in fact, were never satisfactorily resolved by Maunsell and his team.

The overall performance was, however, deemed acceptable for a further 10 locomotives to be ordered for delivery in 1928-9. This order was quickly followed with a further one for five more in 1929, making 16 in all. This last order should have been for 15, but the financial constraints of the time, imposed by the electrification issues, mentioned in the previous Chapter, reduced this by 10. Perhaps the following quote by Harold Holcroft in his classic *Locomotive Adventure* will put matters into perspective:

> When No. E850 went into service in the latter end of 1926, Maunsell thought it advisable to be thoroughly satisfied with its performance before proceeding with more; a full scale test with a train of 520 tons between Waterloo and Exeter confirmed that it was capable of doing so, but it was two years before a batch of 10 were put into service. Then 15 more were asked for in order to share 26 between Nine Elms and Battersea, but the General Manager (Walker) cut it down to five, giving a total of 16, that was eight to each shed and not enough to establish train services of Nelson capacity; therefore they had to be limited to 425 tons so that a 'King Arthur' could take over if a 'Nelson' was not available. Thus the 500 ton loading for which the 'Nelson' was designed to meet never materialised.
>
> The cut in numbers was the result of the Board's decision to embark on main-line electrification. Had the two year's delay in starting to build the 'Nelsons' in quantity not occurred it is probable that a sufficient number would have been completed before the electrification bug bit the management!

It was in 1929 that the smoke deflectors made their appearance, to alleviate complaints from crews of smoke obscuring forward visibility, with Nos. 861 to 865 being fitted with smoke deflectors from new.

Maunsell's health, by the early 1930s, was becoming troublesome and must have affected his work somewhat. Perhaps this is one reason why he did not experiment too much to try and overcome the locomotive's shortcomings, save for the following episodes. No. 859 *Lord Hood* was built with 6 ft 3 in. driving wheels instead of 6 ft 7 in. ones, No. 860 *Lord Hawke* was built with a boiler 10 inches longer than standard, No. 865 *Sir John Hawkins* was modified to the more conventional 90 degree crank setting in 1933, and No. 862 *Lord Collingwood* was fitted with a Kylchap double chimney and multiple blastpipe in August 1934.

None of these changes appeared to provide much of a performance improvement, although in respect of the 90 degree crank setting there is a Stewarts Lane report into coal consumption which showed that this modification apparently caused a 7 per cent increase over that of the standard locomotives. However, there is a record of an outstanding run to Salisbury with the Kylchap No. 862 of 80¾ minutes with a 375 ton load. Involving a speed of 85 mph at Hurstbourne, this is the only known recorded run of the Kylchap-fitted engine and it seems likely that, as the performance of the original was essentially satisfactory to permit the 'Nelsons' to carry out their duties without complaints of poor time-keeping, Maunsell chose to soft-pedal any small improvements that might have appeared. After all, by the mid-1930s he was aware of the approach of retirement which would be occasioned by his age and failing health.

An interesting experiment commenced in 1933 involving the 'Nelson' class, but not implemented until 1937, when No. 857 was fitted with a nickel steel boiler embodying a combustion chamber and round top firebox. The then current project studies made towards a Pacific stretch of the 'Nelson' were proposed, using a nickel steel boiler to save weight due to the thinner plate possible with this high tensile material. Although the stretched version never appeared, No. 857 employed this boiler until it was uneconomic to repair it for further use in about 1945.

One design feature which continued to be used by Maunsell around this time was the construction of wooden mock-ups of the cabs as a guide to incorporating the controls, something which has been done in Aviation for some decades now. This amplifies how far ahead some of his thinking was, as none of the other CME's at that time used such a technique so extensively. The mock-up was not only for the benefit of enginemen, who gave their opinions on the layout as it affected them, but was frequently used by draughtsmen and

'Lord Nelson' class No. 857 *Lord Howe* is seen with the 11.00 am 'Continental' passing Bromley on 30th March, 1938. Note the non-Belpaire boiler, which was scrapped in 1945 when worn out and replaced with a standard spare.   *H.C. Casserley*

'Schools' class No. 902, *Wellington* in original condition without smoke deflectors.

MLS Collection

The first of the second (1932) batch of 'Schools' No. 910 *Merchant Taylors* going well with a Dover express, the carriages of which appear to be Maunsell 'low-window'.   *MLS Collection*

fitters to assess the accessibility for pipe runs etc. in the early stages of design and construction.

But before we continue with the final stage of our survey of Maunsell's career, we need to consider possibly the greatest and most successful of his passenger designs which appeared after the 'Nelsons'. The archetypal British express passenger locomotive has often been thought to be the 4-4-0, and certainly Maunsell was well experienced in this particular type, as we have seen with his sojourn at Inchicore and, subsequently, on the SE&CR at Ashford with the finalisation of the 'L' class in 1914, plus rebuilds of the 'D' and 'E' classes in 1920 and 1921 respectively. This experience was enhanced by his early days as CME of the Southern, when the 'L1' appeared. Certainly, by the mid to late 1920s, Maunsell had had adequate experience covering the design and application in traffic of this classic layout over the Southern routes.

The catalyst for the design which evolved into the successful 'V', or 'Schools' class of 4-4-0, was the requirement by the Traffic Department for a locomotive having an axle load of no more than 21 tons and capable of dealing with 400 ton trains over routes where structural limitations were such that the employment of 'King Arthurs' was not possible. The corresponding average speed required was 55 mph.

The recently introduced 'L1', built in 1926, was initially considered as a starting point, but was ruled out very quickly, as the early studies using this class as a datum very quickly showed that 'stretching' this already 'stretched' type was not an option which could be adopted. Some further exercises were undertaken involving increasing the water capacity of the 'River' class tanks, but the Sevenoaks accident effectively removed that option, which would have created the need for even more permanent way modifications due to the increased weight and, consequently, axle loadings that such design changes would cause. And so it was that Maunsell was forced by circumstances to prepare a completely new design.

The 'Lord Nelson' prototype had just been built and had entered service. So the first serious design study was based on a cut-down 'Nelson', eliminating one of the coupled axles, truncating the boiler and firebox, and having three cylinders instead of four.   However, the axle loading that resulted was 22 tons, in excess of the specified limit. A second iteration was then proposed by Clayton in which the Belpaire firebox favoured by Maunsell was replaced by a round-topped version as employed on the 'King Arthur' class. It probably would have been necessary to employ this type of firebox in any case, as one of the prime routes on which the class was to be used was that from Tonbridge to Hastings via Battle, with its restricted tunnel clearances which entailed raking the cab side profile inwards at the top. A Belpaire box would have restricted the forward vision severely. The round-topped box eliminated this problem. This shaping of the cab sides was a feature unique to the 'Schools'.

In the interests of economy and standardisation, the wheels, bogie, and outside cylinders came from the 'Lord Nelson' class, hence the typical Maunsell inset valve chests as on his other three-cylinder designs were absent. The boiler was a cut-down version of the 'N15' class. One other feature, unique to the

'Schools' class No. 927, *Clifton* on Bournemouth train of all-Maunsell stock, a duty in which they excelled.   *MLS Collection*

'Schools' class No. 936, *Cranleigh*, a particularly sharp picture which gives a good view of the lines of this 4-4-0 design. Maunsell's best, many say.   *MLS Collection*

'Schools' was the fact that this design did not employ the tall front buffer beam common to the 'N1', 'U1', 'W' and 'Z' three cylinder types, as the drive from all cylinders was concentrated on the front axle, which permitted all to be on the same alignment. In this context it appears strange that Maunsell did not consider a conjugated valve gear for the 'Schools', for Holcroft's original schemes had been made on a 4-4-0 design with all cylinders on a common alignment. The complete gear could be fitted to the rear of the valves, thus eliminating the problem of expansion of lengthy linkages on the Mogul layouts, and permitting a compact, easily accessible drive. One can only speculate that he was still worried about the over-run caused by bearing wear, backed by the fact that all previous conjugated gears on the Southern had been replaced with a third set of conventional Walschaerts for precisely this feature.

At 25,130 lb., the 'Schools' had the highest tractive effort of any British 4-4-0, almost equal to that of the 'King Arthur' value, which was 25,320 lb.

From the outset, this new 4-4-0 was a success, handling the sometimes 11 to 12 coach Hastings line expresses with consummate ease in addition to the Charing Cross to Ramsgate fast services. The Hastings route was, in fact, to become the 'Schools' preserve for over a quarter of a century. Between 1930 and 1935 forty of the class were constructed, such was the versatility of the design, which eventually showed its full capability in hauling trains in excess of 500 tons on the Southampton and Bournemouth run, and keeping time in such endeavours.

Maunsell must have been well pleased with the outcome of this last Southern 4-4-0 design. At least it made up for the slightly disappointing 'Lord Nelson' episode, of which further iterations were to be schemed over the years 1931 to 1934.

The first 'Nelson' study involved a four-cylinder compound variant which externally was identical to the baseline design, employing the same boiler pressed to 250 psi. The high pressure cylinders were 15½ in. and low pressure 22 in., both having strokes of 26 in. The tractive effort remained unchanged at 33,500 lb. This design remained on the board, even though authority to convert one of the existing fleet was obtained. This experimental version was intended to employ poppet valves, a current development being tried by Gresley and Bulleid on various LNER locomotives. In 1933, a stretched 'Nelson' appeared in the form of a 4-6-2 Pacific, employing 6 ft 3 in. wheels, and a stretched boiler of 220 psi pressure with a wide firebox, similar to that employed by Gresley. This particular study was an additional iteration on the earlier Compound mentioned above, which had retained the narrow firebox of the baseline locomotive. The cylinders were 16 in. in diameter and stroke was 26 in. The resulting tractive effort came out at 33,190 lb. Again this design never progressed beyond the project stage, largely it seems due to the length and axle loading restricting it to relatively few routes.

This was not the end of the story, however, as Maunsell turned his ever active mind to the consideration of an express Beyer Garratt instead of a Pacific, largely on the grounds of the moderate axle loading possible with such a layout. The Pacific study provided the power units, except that the four cylinders of this project were changed to three. The final layout was of the 4-6-2 + 2-6-4 type. Of 209 tons weight and 100 ft in length, these were enormous locomotives to consider on the Southern, which the Civil Engineer refused to accept on the

Eastern Section and only permitted them to operate between Basingstoke and Exeter. According to a Traffic Department study carried out on Maunsell's instructions, the employment of 10 Garratts would enable 64 conventional locomotives to be deployed elsewhere. However, many of the displaced engines would have been called back on the holiday weekends to cope with the West of England expresses which often ran as three to five separate trains to cope with demand. Had the Garratt been cleared into Waterloo, there would have been problems with train lengths fouling the platform exit points if it had been used to its full potential. The project went as far as Beyer, Peacock & Co. being asked to quote for the 10 locomotives, only for the proposal to be rejected by the Board.

As 1935 approached, Maunsell was beset with increasing ill-health, which incapacitated him considerably during that year. He was away for some weeks due to this illness, and Pearson had to deputise for him at Board meetings, necessitating frequent trips up to Waterloo for briefing on Agenda items concerning the CME's office. In December Richard underwent an operation in hospital, which resulted in convalescence until March the following year. On the 12th December Clayton was appointed acting CME by Sir Herbert Walker until further notice. Much work was delegated out to the by now ageing but very experienced, team and engineering matters moved on smoothly in the design offices under Clayton until Maunsell returned to take up the reins again on 4th March, 1935. Hooley was still busily engaged on scheming yet further express types, producing no fewer than four different designs of 2-6-2 tender locomotives. However, the continued opposition to pony trucks for express use still emanated from Ellson's office in the Civil Engineering Department, so these proposals were fated from the start and died on the drawing board.

As the final batch of 'Schools' was emerging from Eastleigh in 1935 in the midst of all these project studies for more express types, Maunsell had turned his ideas towards the forthcoming need to replace and add to the ageing 0-6-0 freight types, the youngest of which were the ex-LB&SC class 'C3' of 1906. So, as we approach the closing years of his working life, we shall examine the reasons behind the need to bolster up the freight motive power and how Richard set his mind to this, in addition to introducing the new technology associated with diesel-electric power.

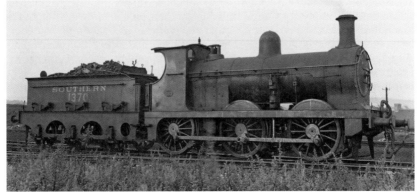

'O1' class No. 1370 (Wainwright) which, despite its careworn appearance in 1935, lived on until 1960!   *J.H.L. Adams*

Chapter Twelve

The Freight Side of Things
and Retirement

As we have seen, the Southern Railway goods and freight work remained the domain of steam in parallel with the extensive electrification of both suburban and main lines. There was the problem of the live rail not being suitable for use in goods yards, presenting too much of a hazard to shunters and other staff. So, until the advent of diesel-electric or diesel units, the Southern was committed to retaining steam for goods work. The passenger side of business provided some three-quarters of the traffic receipts, and it was logical and sensible to feed the majority of investment into this. Coupled with the limited funding was the scarcity of heavy industry in those areas served by the Southern, which reduced the freight needs, when compared with the other railways. Large amounts of freight services were transient, in that they fed through the system to the other main lines, or from other lines into and through the Southern to the Channel ports. Whilst some of the coal for its locomotives was obtained locally from the Kent coalfields, a considerable amount was still imported from Wales, the Midlands and the North. The port of Southampton was an important point of import and export, and had been extensively developed by the owners, firstly the London and South Western Railway and then, after Grouping, the Southern Railway, to maximise the business potential. Considerable movements of agricultural goods, many of them seasonal, emanated from Kent, Wiltshire, Dorset, Somerset, Devon, the Isle of Wight and the Channel Islands.

The most important of the large freight depots owned and run by the Southern were in London; Nine Elms (ex-LSWR) and Bricklayers Arms (combining the ex-LB&SCR and SE&CR terminals). These were fed, in the main, from the Feltham marshalling yard, which sorted out the traffic for London from the exchanges to or from other railways. In addition Norwood yard dealt with the Central area and Hither Green the Eastern area.

Considerable exchange traffic took place at points such as Salisbury, Basingstoke, Templecombe, Andover, Exeter and Plymouth, these being the major connections to the other railways which bordered the Southern's domain. All-in-all, the Southern's freight services were certainly important enough to warrant the continued development of suitable motive power to maintain and increase their level as the country clambered out of recession and towards the next World War.

The year 1927 saw some new mixed traffic locomotives appearing, in the shape of fifteen 'S15' class 4-6-0s, which were very similar to a 'King Arthur' but with 5 ft 7 in. diameter coupled wheels, a shorter firebox, and consequently detail differences to the motion. The features embodied in Maunsell's redesign of the original 'N15' coupled with the Urie 'S15' reliability, produced a very useful mixed traffic type, capable of much useful work on the passenger side when seasonal demands on such workings were heavy. The 20 original Urie types continued unmodified, and could be easily distinguished by their cab, lack of outside steam pipes and raised running plates over the cylinders. For

'S15' class No. 841, of the 1936 batch.

MLS Collection

'S15' No. 847 as preserved and running on the 3.30 pm ex-Sheffield Park on 27th April, 1997. A purely Maunsell scene, with the restored rake of Maunsell coaches making up the train.

Author

Maunsell's versions of the 'S15', not so apparent was the raising of boiler pressure to 200 lb./sq. in from 180 lb./sq. in. and the reduction of cylinder diameter by half an inch to 20 in., these modifications combining to raise the tractive effort to 29,860 lb., an increase of 2,610 lb. over the Urie version.

The success of the 'S15' design led to a further 10 being built to the same specification in 1936, bringing the total of the class to 45. The improvements introduced by Maunsell were so effective as to permit the continuation of manufacture of what had been considered by some an obsolete design. It was also cost-effective, in that much of the original tooling was already available for re-use.

The 'S15s' and mixed-traffic Moguls, whilst covering much of the longer range freight hauls and fast goods services, were not meant to cover the smaller goods runs, used to deliver a wide range of materials to local sidings and goods yards. This type of service was covered to a great extent by the ubiquitous 0-6-0 tender types.

In the early 1930s, Maunsell had ordered some studies into a 4-8-0 freight locomotive for the longer hauls, but its limited route availability effectively killed any chance of it appearing. Recourse to the existing designs was the best option for this requirement.

We now need to consider briefly the state of the 0-6-0 fleet on the Southern in 1935-6 to fully appreciate the reasoning behind the decision to replace the older locomotives with the modern 'Q' class. *Table Four* lists the totals of all 0-6-0 tender types that entered the Southern stock at Grouping, and compares it with the situation in 1935. It can be seen that the youngest class was the 'C3' of 1906, discounting the fragmented rebuilding programme of the 'C2' into the 'C2X'.

Table Four

Southern 0-6-0 Tender types to 1935

Class	First built	Into SR stock at Grouping	No. in service by 1935
B1/B2	1877	8	-
C	1900	109	109
O	1878	29	-
O1	1903*	57	56
C1	1882	1	-
C2	1893	55	43
C2X	1908†	32	42
C3	1906	10	10
0278	1872	6	-
0302	1874	15	-
0395	1881	20	20
700	1897	30	30
	Totals	372	310

Notes: * Rebuilds of 'O' class. † Rebuilding of the 'C2' to 'C2X' continued from 1908 to 1940, and had reached this stage by 1935.

The 'B1', 'B2', 'O', 'C1', '0278' and '0302' classes were all scrapped shortly after entering SR stock.

Wainwright 'C' class 0-6-0, the most numerous of all Southern freight types. This one, originally No. 61 in SE&CR days, lasted for 61 years in service.   *J.H.L. Adams*

An example of the class 'C2X', rebuilt over the years of Maunsell's reign. No. 2538 has been captured at Tunbridge Wells West on 20th September, 1947.   *J.M. Jarvis*

Although many of the withdrawn 0-6-0s had been replaced by the mixed-traffic Moguls, continual withdrawal of further ageing 0-6-0 classes was taking place and the fleet of such types was shrinking. When we look at a fleet of slightly over 370 in 1923, this pales into insignificance when we realise that the LNWR, MR and L&YR had bequeathed between them nearly 3,000 to the LMS in the same year.

In goods parlance, the 0-6-0 was, perhaps, the archetypal British locomotive built in large numbers by all the railways for over 80 years. To Richard Maunsell, it must have seemed logical to continue the perpetuity of this classic and versatile layout. And so the 'Q' class was born. Hooley was given the task of laying out the design as early as 1934-5. Tragically he was not to see this locomotive authorised as, during 1935 he was taken seriously ill several times and died suddenly on 12th January, 1936, just a few weeks before the authorisation came through for 20 examples. The 'Q' design was to be Maunsell's last steam design for the Southern.

Unmistakably Maunsell in styling it employed much of the 'N' and 'L1' in its makeup. The 3,500 gallon tenders came from 'U' class locomotives which were being re-equipped with 4,000 gallon units. The Belpaire firebox, so popular with Richard, returned. Steam reversing was employed together with valve gear operated by the Stephenson link motion. It was also the first, and only, Maunsell design to employ outside admission valves, which offer a freer exhaust passage. This latter feature was brought about following an incident at Eastleigh, where he was firstly regaled with a treatise on outside admission valves by a member of his technical staff, Eric Forge, who then managed to persuade him to mount a shaky trestle in the erecting shop and peer down the blastpipe of a 'D15' 4-4-0 undergoing general repair. It was possible to see straight into the cylinders, and the virtues of a free exhaust were immediately apparent. Maunsell said nothing at the time, but when he departed he said, 'Thank you, Forge, that was very interesting. You have made your point'.

Production of the 'Q' did not commence until after Maunsell had retired, and the first 11 were delivered from Eastleigh in 1938 with the balance of nine coming in 1939, again from Eastleigh.

From the outset there were two main problems with the 'Q'. The first of these was that of poor steaming qualities, which after the success of the Moguls appears puzzling, particularly as these had been excellent steamers ever since they appeared. It was not until 1955 that the steaming problem was tackled successfully, with trials at the then British Railways test plant at Swindon. The cure was simply to fit the standard BR class '4' blastpipe and a stovepipe chimney, which worked like a charm. The writer cannot help wondering whether the steaming problems were allied to the second complaint which revolved around the Stephenson valve gear. The differing exhaust freedom, when compared to the Walschaerts' gear, combined with the blast-pipe diameter, outside admission valves and chimney choke of the original design may have been partly responsible for this poor steaming. Be that as it may, the remedy only came as the end of steam approached. However, nine of the class were modified in 1958, even though withdrawals began in 1962. The whole class was gone by 1965.

Maunsell's answer to the 0-6-0 replacement need, class 'Q'. No. 535 is seen standing outside Eastleigh shed.

The preserved example of Maunsell's 'Q' class is seen in the yard at Sheffield Park on 24th September, 1987. *M. Frackeiwicz*

Returning to the Stephenson valve gear, there were complaints of mechanical reliability problems allied to this fit, presumably associated with a feature of its layout. Stephenson valve gear, for so long beloved by Churchward on the GWR, was noted for its ability to provide a good strong pulling power at low speed, a feature which would be of advantage in accelerating heavy goods trains to their moderate transit speeds. However, it requires two eccentrics for each valve as compared to the normal single eccentric of the Walschaerts' gear. This can leave less room for substantial journals on the axle of inside cylinder locomotives and lead to the mechanical problems of wear occasioned by hard pulling at low speed for long periods, which usually manifests itself in hot boxes. Many of Maunsell's contemporaries stated that Stephenson gear was a retrograde step and it was certainly the first employment of this type of valve gear by Maunsell on a wholly new design for the Southern.

As has already been said, Maunsell was retired by the time the 'Q' entered service, under the CME leadership of Oliver Bulleid, who instigated some trials with various blast-pipes and chimneys on one of the class, but without success. He was obviously on the right track, as we have already seen the remedy did lie in a particular combination of these items, but Bulleid did not find the right one in his rather 'hit and miss' approach. One example of this final Maunsell steam design has been preserved and is to be found on the Bluebell Railway.

The last locomotive design associated with Richard Maunsell was neither steam nor electric, but what was to become a major type of prime mover in later years, the diesel-electric concept. Following the provision of specialised shunting tank locomotives typified by the 'Z' 0-8-0T design, his attention was drawn to the potential of employing diesel-electric units in shunting yards, as typified by the LMS experiments in 1932 with Armstrong-Whitworth and English Electric units. These experiments were so successful that in 1934 twenty more units, with increased engine power, had been ordered by the LMS from Armstrong-Whitworth. Capable of 24-hour operation, carrying fuel for a week's operations, they were an immediate success in the yards. Never one to neglect the advances in railway technology, Maunsell, whilst the 'Q' was being designed, instigated a study into the feasibility of using diesel-electric units in the Southern marshalling yards. Following this he received clearance to order three 0-6-0 units for trials. Industrial pressure at the time meant that there was no manufacturer capable of delivering them before 1939. However, the English Electric Co. Ltd did offer the supply of diesel-electric power units in 1937 providing that the Southern Railway could supply the body and framing themselves.

Ashford accordingly built the three shells and chassis to designs from Eastleigh which were delivered to the Preston works of English Electric for final assembly. The illustration shows the first example being marshalled in the yard opposite Ashford works, minus the coupling rods, for transit to Preston by goods train and the subsequent installation of the power units. In August 1937 the first two units were delivered back to the Southern, followed by the third in September. They were immediately put into service at Norwood yard, operating virtually non-stop for six days a week and proved an immediate success. Some limited use on short distance, light freight services was also

350 hp diesel-electric No. 1 after construction at Ashford works in 1937, being marshalled into a goods train for transfer to English Electric at Preston for the installation of the power train. Note the lack of coupling rods, removed for the journey.   *D.B. Barnard*

undertaken, again with considerable success, although the 350 hp of the units obviously placed limitations on train weights for this type of use.

So, as the Southern entered the field of internal combustion motive power, Maunsell began preparations for his retirement which had now been agreed and announced, together with that of Sir Herbert Walker, in *The Times* on 28th May.

Speculation as to the successor was allayed during the Directors' tour of the West of England facilities of the Southern on 9th June. Richard, who was there as usual, was seen in the company of O.V.S. Bulleid from the LNER, who had been given the all clear by Sir Nigel Gresley, his immediate superior, to consider the post.

On 31st October, 1937 Richard formally handed over the responsibilities of the department to his successor, Oliver Bulleid, who had been appointed and installed on the 20th September, followed by a short familiarisation period, at Waterloo. Sir Herbert Walker had retired shortly before, ending a lifetime of railway management, leaving a profitable organisation which had successfully combated the competition of road transport in the South East of England. Walker and Maunsell had always got on well in their top management capacities, despite the limitations on capital expenditure on locomotive stock caused by the electrification programme. Like all good managers they recognised each other's talents and ensured that their respective disciplines worked to the best advantage together, to the benefit of the complex public service by which they were employed.

On the day before his retirement Richard Maunsell was requested to present himself, together with his wife, at the Charing Cross Hotel for a farewell from 250 representatives of his staff. George Pearson took the chair in his capacity of Assistant Chief Mechanical Engineer and opened the proceedings with a summary of Maunsell's career since 1913 with the South Eastern & Chatham and Southern railways. He paid tribute to Richard's capability as engineer and organiser, also his capacity for hard work. His willingness to help his staff where possible, even at an inconvenience to himself, was also recorded. James Clayton then spoke on behalf of the Technical staff and emphasised Maunsell's activities on the design of rolling stock which was considered to be amongst the best in the country, and stated that the Directors had made a wise choice in appointing him as Chief Mechanical Engineer at Grouping in 1923. Clayton also said that Maunsell's impressive figure would be missed around Waterloo and the works he visited on a regular basis, and concluded with the thanks of all the Technical staff for the help and guidance they had received.

The clerical staff were represented by Mr W. Marsh, who endorsed all the earlier remarks by Messrs Pearson and Clayton. Further speeches from the representatives of the supervisory staff (Mr H.R.C. Corbin) and Locomotive Running Department (Mr A. Cobb) followed, the former stating that his department always appreciated the fact that Maunsell had regarded them as experts in their own area and had depended upon them for advice in many aspects. If that advice was not acted upon, they at least realised that their views had had full consideration. Although a hard taskmaster, Mr Maunsell had known their capabilities and they gave loyal service to one who was of a high standard himself and, as such, greatly admired.

Mr Cobb passed on the good wishes of his staff for the 24 years of association since those first days at Ashford in 1913, and concluded by wishing Mr Maunsell many happy years of retirement with Mrs Maunsell.

At this point in the proceedings Mr Pearson presented an album of remembrance from the CME staff and that of the Locomotive Running Superintendent. This contained an illuminated address, photographs and drawings of locomotives, carriages and wagons constructed during Maunsell's time on the Southern and also photographs of the Technical, Clerical and Supervisory staffs grouped according to their place of work. Mrs Maunsell was then presented with a gold brocade evening bag by Mr Pearson with the good wishes of the staff.

Following a rendering of 'For he's a jolly good fellow' from all present, Maunsell rose to reply. He hoped that the rather lavish eulogies which had been expressed about himself would not be put down to gross exaggeration but only justified exuberance. If he had remained in service a few months more, he would have reached 50 years of continuous railway service, and in regard to his time on the SE&CR and Southern Railway this had always been pleasurable thanks to those working with him having given their assistance so readily. The results of his Department's efforts had only been possible due to loyalty, co-operation and team work of those behind him.

Then singling out those who had spoken before him, he stated that he never had heard Mr Pearson speak at such length before, whilst he was sure that Mr

The Ashford farewell, 1937. Pearson giving his address. *Left to right*: C.J. Hicks (Assistant Works manager), - - Noble, Mrs Hicks, G.H. Pearson, H.J. Tonkin (cost accountant), R.E.L. Maunsell, - - Tarrant (stores supt), J.Palmer (chief draughtsman), Mrs Maunsell, - - Western (Cost Office), H. Chittenden (chief clerk), Bert Banks (Electrical).   *D.B. Barnard*

Ashford Erecting Shop staff, 1937. Photograph taken for insertion into commemorative book presented to Maunsell on his retirement.   *H.M. Dannatt*

Clayton was the 'silver-tongued' orator of the Department and had been, from the early days at Ashford, one who had, from time to time, restrained his Celtic enthusiasm and led him away from 'those danger paths, where it is said, even angels fear to tread'.

After paying tribute to the clerical staff, Maunsell went on to thank the support of the shop foremen and supervisors, without whose common sense, tact and abilities the smooth running of the Workshops and Outdoor Departments would not have been possible. In conclusion he thanked all who came under those who had spoken for their loyalty and co-operation over many years and went on to single out Messrs Pearson, Turbett, Gardener, Hicks and Munns for especial thanks.

Finally, he thanked all present for the album which would remind him of their past work together in his retirement. He also expressed the thanks of Mrs Maunsell for the gift they had presented to her, adding that in her own quiet way, she had taken considerable interest in the welfare of the Department.

The meeting then closed after all present had been invited to have tea by Mr Maunsell.

On 4th November, a further presentation was made to Maunsell by the Ashford staff, who assembled in one of the shops before lunch. A further album, containing an address, group photographs of all the Chief Mechanical Engineer's Department and associated Departments at Ashford works. Also handed over was a case of pipes for Richard and a handbag for Edith, who was present.

Thus ended the reign of the Southern's first CME, after almost 14 years of effort involving the modernising of the steam locomotive stock, now consisting of 1,852 locomotives of 77 classes. Electrification had expanded from purely suburban to suburban and main line use, a policy which was set to continue, halted only by the forthcoming War, throughout the remainder of the Southern's days and into the Nationalisation era. New technology, in the form of diesel-electric locomotives had arrived and the railway was in good shape for the traumatic events which were to enfold it just two years hence.

Ashford must have held some pleasant memories for Richard, as on retirement he negotiated for and purchased the old CME's house at Ashford, 'Northbrooke', in which he had lived during his time there, as CME of the SE&CR and Southern. It had passed into the hands of, and was still owned by, the Southern, and they were only too happy to see their old CME remain there. Here he settled into retirement and relaxed following a busy and auspicious career. In 1938 the Institution of Mechanical Engineers elected him to Honorary Member status, a privilege reserved for none but the most eminent of their membership.

His position in the local community was further enhanced in his latter years by his involvement in the life of the Parish Church, which he and Edith had attended regularly in their time at Ashford. He was elected as a sidesman and was often seen at services organising the collection, often passing the bag around himself. His organisational abilities were often called into play during Parochial Church Council meetings to beneficial effect.

'Northbrooke', the house Maunsell bought from the Southern Railway on his retirement.
Author's Collection

Maunsell's grave in Bybrook cemetery, Ashford.   *J.H. Blackford/Author's Collection*

To return briefly to Richard Maunsell's influence at Inchicore, his design expertise built up in the two years he spent in charge there lived on there for many years, particularly during the rebuilds of the Coey 4-4-0s, which took place during the 1929s and 1930s. We have already seen, in Chapter Four, that these rebuilds were very reminiscent of the single example of Maunsell's Irish 4-4-0 expertise, No. 341, in their styling of running plate, the change to a Belpaire box and the cab shape modifications. One can almost see the Maunsell hand at work. In addition, in the late 1930s, as Richard entered his retirement, the design office at Inchicore was busy scheming a new and powerful express 4-6-0. Much has been said about the close resemblance between the LMS 'Royal Scot', in its rebuilt guise, and this locomotive, the '800' class, but it should also be noted that the 'Royal Scot' was itself derived from Maunsell's own 'Lord Nelson' as we have seen in Chapter Eleven. So, it appears that Richard could have looked favourably on this tenuous, but definite, link with his own design expertise in the early years of his retirement. The '800' class, the largest and most powerful locomotive ever built in Ireland, was restricted to just three members, and one, *Maedhbh*, is preserved for posterity at the Ulster Transport Museum at Cultra, Co. Down. Sadly, none of Maunsell's Irish creations are preserved in his native land, even though most of them lived on until the end of steam in Ireland.

Richard kept in touch with those of his pupils still training at Ashford, they often were seen to visit 'Northbrooke' to acquaint their former master of their progress. Although coming under the remit of Oliver Bulleid, these pupils were used to the weekly progress meetings instigated by Maunsell, and found it hard to adjust to a monthly meeting as required by Bulleid. Richard had always placed great emphasis on the regular contact with his pupils, to encourage them as they climbed the ladder in their careers on the railway, an important fact which had been instilled into him during his time under Ivatt and Aspinall in the 1880s and 1890s.

Some visits to the old Waterloo office were made, primarily to see Holcroft, who, in 1939, took Richard to see the last improvements to the running sheds at Stewarts Lane, which had been approved by him a few weeks prior to retirement. Holcroft had stayed on under Bulleid to give some continuity to the design progress, although this new incumbent very soon had matters completely altered to his own requirements appearing during World War II in the shape of the 'Q1' and 'Merchant Navy' classes with their unorthodox construction and technical features.

In 1942, his health was becoming more frail, and he made his last Will, making provision for any grandchildren that might ensue from daughter Netta's marriage in the event of her predeceasing them. After some pecuniary bequests to family and friends, the bulk of the estate was to go to Edith. Richard's distinctive signature confirmed the document.

Little more is known about the years of retirement, except that Maunsell stayed at the Ashford house until his death on 7th March, 1944, resolutely refusing to move from an area which was in the thick of the early years of conflict. The funeral was a quiet affair, with the state of events locally, as the country prepared for the forthcoming invasion of Europe. His last known public appearance was at the Dover harbour centenary celebrations on 7th February, 1944. Edith lived on for just over a further year, dying on 11th March, 1945, and is buried with Richard in the Bybrook Cemetery, Ashford, a few hundred yards from the house 'Northbrooke' which had been their home for 32 years.

'Northbrooke' passed into the hands of Netta and her husband, Commander Slade, who remained living there until the end of their lives. They had no family, so when Commander Slade died the house and all that was in it went to a niece of his living in America, who came over to dispose of the property and contents. By some quirk of fate, this niece asked a retired railwayman, Mr G.M. Rial, what to do with the piles of archives found in the attic. He offered to go through them and retain any that might be of interest for transmission to the National Railway Museum. This is how the archives currently at York came to be preserved and became the catalyst for the production of this book. If this had not happened, then the story of an eminent Irish engineer who rose to the top of his profession could not have been told, and the memory of his exploits would have been restricted purely to those of his locomotives as remain in preservation. Fine they may be, but they cannot tell the story of how their creator aquired his expertise and worked with and moulded the ideas of his team into some great examples of Irish and British railways' motive power.

This paperweight model of 'King Arthur' class No. 763 was rescued from the attic of 'Northbrooke'.   *G.M. Rial*

Appendix One

The Inchicore Speeches, 1896

Congratulatory Address to R.E.L. Maunsell made at reception and dinner for Messrs Coey and Maunsell, Inchicore Works, 11th April, 1896

To R.E.L. Maunsell Esq.

Sir,

We the employees of the Locomotive Department of the Great Southern and Western Railway, bid you a hearty welcome amongst us once more.

We also desire you to accept our congratulations on your appointment to the important position as Manager of the Inchicore Works.

This position having been held by men, who from it, have obtained the greatest honors the railway world can bestow, we beg therefore to remind you of the pleasure we feel in recognising that it is now held for the first time by one who is possessed of the two-fold advantage of being an Irishman and a graduate of our own works. We can assure you that we will not fail to redouble our energies, so as to make the work allotted to us worthy of the Management of our Fellow Countryman.

We feel assured from your high qualifications and intelligence that you will adopt the noble principles so ably pursued by your predecessor of encouraging Irish industry and the welfare of those employed in every possible moment.

In conclusion we wish you prosperity and happiness and hope to see you in the near future a 'Leading Light' in Railway engineering.

We have the honor to Remain
Your well devoted Servants
Signed on behalf of The Employees
11th April 1896

Maunsell's reply to the Congratulatory Address

Mr Chairman, Mr Vice-Chairman & Gentlemen,

I have listened to the address that the Honorary Secretary of your Committee has just now read with feelings of great pleasure and not a little pride. But at the same time and in fact since first I heard of your kindly intention to recognise the occasion of Mr Coey's promotion to the post of Locomotive Superintendent and my return among you in so graceful and hearty a manner as you are now doing, I have had very grave doubts of my capability to make a suitable reply. It is usually taken for granted that because a man is Irish he can rattle off a speech without the least difficulty. Well, whatever the Goddess of Blarney, or whoever or whatever that power may be who presides over the art of oratory, may have done for others, she has certainly neglected me sadly. Speaking technically, she has left me just as I came from the mould, and has not even taken the trouble to have me fettled. It is impossible for me to thank you sufficiently for the beautiful address with which you have presented me, congratulating me on my appointment as Works Manager, and welcoming me back again among you. It seems to me only like yesterday since I left Inchicore and joined the L&YR, but in reality it is considerably over six years. Since then I have travelled over a good portion of the World and have had an opportunity of seeing how our fellow country-men live and how Railway work is conducted in other countries under different circumstances. But after all, I have come to the conclusion that there is no place like home, and I need scarcely tell you I am very glad indeed to be back again in the old country and in the old works where I served my time as a lad, and how fully I appreciate the honour our Directors have conferred on me by appointing me to be Mr Coey's successor. Now perhaps some of you may not recognise at first sight the importance of that term successor, but when you analyse it, you begin to appreciate what vast obligations it lays on the man who 'succeeds'. Apart from many other considerations and speaking generally, it means that when a man is promoted to a higher sphere, his successor is expected to be capable to carry on his work in an equally efficient manner and if possible to improve on it. Now looking at the subject in this light, I think you will agree with me that my work is pretty well cut. Mr Coey is too well known to you all, both as a thoroughly practical and scientific Mechanical Engineer for anything I can say to raise him higher in your estimation. I can only say that I am proud to have been the one selected to work directly under him and I trust that in time he will find me a useful and capable assistant. I can safely promise him he will find me a loyal one. In your address you express the hope that I will continue in the same line as my predecessors, and discharge my duties in a manner similar to that in which they have discharged theirs. Gentlemen, let me assure you that in this you have not only given expression to my most earnest desire. Any other course of action, would, I am convinced prove detrimental to the interests of the Railway Coy, and to your interests and to my own. I know we are all proud of our shops at Inchicore, and of the work that we turn out of them. Our Works are far and away the finest of their kind in Ireland and as regards the quality of the work we turn out, we can hold our own with any of the large Railway shops. Our rolling stock is in first class condition and I can safely say that we have not a single engine running that can be termed in a bad state of repair. This excellent state of affairs is entirely due to the unflagging energy and the solid hard work of the gentlemen you refer to as my predecessors, namely, Mr McDonnell, Mr Aspinall, Mr Ivatt and Mr Coey, and their subordinates, and I think you will agree with me that it would be a very shortsighted policy on my part to attempt any radical changes in a system that has proved so thoroughly satisfactory. The positions that have been, and are still being held by these gentlemen since they left Inchicore is, to my mind, conclusive evidence that their efforts and work were appreciated, not only by our Directors, but by the Directors of other Railway Companies. Now I have said a little in praise of Inchicore, and I feel that it is justly deserved, but there are two sides to every question, and I do not wish you for a moment to run away with the idea, or to imagine that I am satisfied that Inchicore is perfect and incapable of further improvement or development. A gentleman whose opinion I respect highly said to me a short time ago that once the people connected with a place get the idea into their heads that their place is perfect and needs no improvement, it is a certain sign that that place is going to the dogs. I must say I entirely agree with him, and I go further and say that what applies to communities, in this respect, is equally applicable to individuals. It is both your duty and mine not to be contented with the small amount of knowledge we managed to scrape together when we were serving our times and since, but to take advantage of every opportunity to improve ourselves and to keep pace with the times. We resemble a ship in mid ocean, for even if we wish to we cannot drop our anchors and remain stationary. We must keep up our fires or else steam will drop and in a short time, instead of going ahead, we will find ourselves drifting astern. I am conscious that at present, I am wanting in many respects of that accurate knowledge of details which it is absolutely necessary for a Works Manager to possess, but I am determined, by degrees, to become familiar with those details, and thus make my services as useful and valuable as possible to my Employers, and inspire you with a greater degree of confidence in me. Before I conclude let me again thank you warmly and sincerely for the beautiful address with which you have presented me and for the hearty reception you have given me this evening. Also for your assurances that I, who have been placed in my present official position by a vote in which you had no voice, am welcome among you, and that it is your desire and intention to assist me as far as lies in your power. With such assurances I feel that half my battle is already won, and that the remainder depends entirely on my own energies and application, and my earnest wish is that when my day of reckoning comes you will all be able to say that whatever else my shortcomings might have been, you always received strict justice and impartiality from me.

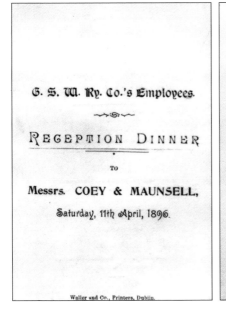

G. S. W. Ry. Co.'s Employees.

RECEPTION DINNER

TO

Messrs. COEY & MAUNSELL,

Saturday, 11th April, 1896.

Waller and Co., Printers, Dublin.

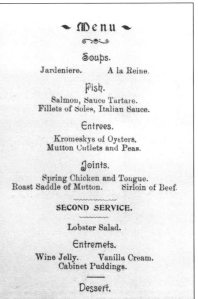

Menu

Soups.

Jardeniere. A la Reine.

Fish.

Salmon, Sauce Tartare.
Fillets of Soles, Italian Sauce.

Entrees.

Kromeskys of Oysters.
Mutton Cutlets and Peas.

Joints.

Spring Chicken and Tongue.
Roast Saddle of Mutton. Sirloin of Beef.

SECOND SERVICE.

Lobster Salad.

Entremets.

Wine Jelly. Vanilla Cream.
Cabinet Puddings.

Dessert.

Appendix Two

Maunsell Locomotives 1912-1937

Class	Type Prototype	First batch batches	Subsequent	Total built
GS&WR				
341	4-4-0	1912 (P)	-	1
257	0-6-0	1913	1914	8
L2*	0-4-2T	1914	-	1
SE&CR				
L†	4-4-0	1914	-	22
K	2-6-4T	1917 (P)	1925-6	20
N	2-6-0	1917 (P)	1920-2	12
E1	4-4-0	1919	1920	11
D1	4-4-0	1921	1920-27	21
SR				
N	2-6-0	1923	1924-34	68
N1	2-6-0	1922 (P)	1930	6
N15	4-6-0	1925-6	1926-7	54
N15X#	4-6-0	1934-6	-	7
S15	4-6-0	1927-8	1936	25
L1	4-4-0	1926	-	15
LN	4-6-0	1926 (P)	1928-9	16
Z	0-8-0T	1929	-	8
V	4-4-0	1930	1932-5	40
U	2-6-0	1917 (as K)	1925-31§	50
U1	2-6-0	1925 (P) (as K1)	1931	21
W	2-6-4T	1931-2	1935-6	15
Q	0-6-0	1938-9	-	20

Notes
* Replacement for the 1875 design of McDonnell, used as works shunter at Inchicore until the 1960s.
† Completion of outstanding Wainwright design.
§ 1925-6 batch as Class K (River) 2-6-4T, rebuilt as U.
# Rebuilt from ex-LBSCR Billinton class 'L' 4-6-4T.
(P) Denotes prototype.

Maunsell Preserved Locomotives

Class	Type	No.	Built	Withdrawn	Now found at
U	2-6-0	1618	1928	1964	Bluebell Rly
U	2-6-0	1806 *	1928	1964	Mid-Hants Rly
U	2-6-0	1625	1929	1964	Mid-Hants Rly
U	2-6-0	1638	1931	1964	Bluebell Rly
S15	4-6-0	841	1936	1964	N. Yorks Moor Rly
S15	4-6-0	847	1936	1964	Bluebell Rly
S15	4-6-0	828	1927	1964	Eastleigh
S15	4-6-0	825 †	1927	1964	N. Yorks Moor Rly
S15	4-6-0	830	1927	1964	Bluebell Rly
N	2-6-0	1874	1925	1964	Mid-Hants Rly
N15	4-6-0	777	1925	1961	NRM, York
Q	0-6-0	54	1939	1965	Bluebell Rly
V	4-4-0	925	1934	1962	NRM, York
V	4-4-0	926	1934	1962	N. Yorks Moor Rly
V	4-4-0	928	1934	1962	Bluebell Rly
LN	4-6-0	850	1926	1962	Carnforth

Notes

*   Rebuilt from 'River' class 2-6-4T.

†   Boiler removed for use in Urie S15 No 506 on Mid Hants Rly. Frames and wheels taken to Shipyard Services for new all-welded boiler.

(N.B. Although the 'S15' was a Urie design, the locomotives listed here were built under Maunsell, with appropriate modifications.)

Examples of the 'W' and 'Z' classes were held over for the National Collection, but this scheme was later reversed and they were scrapped.

'S15' class 4-6-0 No. 847 approaches Three Arch Bridge with the 12.37 pm from Sheffield Park on the Bluebell Railway on 19th March, 1995.   *M. Frackiewicz*

Bibliography

Archives, Trinity University, Dublin
Archives, The Royal School, Armagh
Proceedings of the Institution of Mechanical Engineers
Proceedings of the Institution of Locomotive Engineers
Southern Railway Magazine
Maunsell Archives, National Railway Museum
150 Years of Irish Railways by Fergus Mulligan (Appletree Press)
'Anglo-Irish Connection' by Philip Atkins
Ashford Works Centenary 1847-1947 (Southern Railway publication)
A Pictorial Record of Southern Locomotives by J.H. Russell (OPC)
British Locomotives of the 20th Century by O.S. Nock (PSL)
Bulleid of the Southern by H.A.V. Bulleid (Ian Allan)
Crewe Locomotive Works by Brian Reed [for account of court action to prevent
    LNWR building locos for LYR] (David & Charles)
Experiments with Steam by C. Fryer (PSL)
Historic Railway Disasters by O.S. Nock (Ian Allan)
Irish Railways in Colour by Tom Ferris (Midland Publishing)
Irish Standard Gauge Railways by Tom Middlemass
Irish Steam by O.S. Nock (David & Charles)
Leader and Southern Experimental Steam by Kevin Robertson (Alan Sutton)
Locomotive Adventure by Harold Holcroft (Ian Allan)
Manuscript Sources for the History of Irish Civilisation by R.J. Hayes
Master Builders of Steam by H.A.V. Bulleid (Ian Allan)
Maunsell Locomotives by Brian Haresnape (Ian Allan)
Maunsell's Nelsons by D.W. Winkworth (George Allen & Unwin)
Maunsell's SR Steam Carriage Stock by David Gould (Oakwood Press)
On and Off the Rails by Sir John Elliot (George Allen & Unwin)
Railway Liveries 1923-1947 by Brian Haresnape (Ian Allan)
'Reminiscences of an Irish Locomotive Works' by E.E. Joynt, *The Locomotive*, 1932-3
Royal Trains by Patrick Kingston (Guild Publishing)
'Some Inchicore Proposals' by R.N. Clements (Jnl IRRS Oct. 1973)
Southern Steam by O.S. Nock (David & Charles)
SR 150 by D. St John Thomas & P. Whitehouse (Guild Publishing)
Steam from Waterloo by Col H.C.B.Rogers (David & Charles)
That was my Railway by Frank L. Hick (Silver Link)
The Aspinall Era by H.A.V. Bulleid (Ian Allan)
The British Steam Locomotive, 1925-65 by O.S. Nock (Ian Allan)
The Drummond Greyhounds of the LSWR by D.L. Bradley (Ian Allan)
The Great Southern and Western Railway by Kevin Murray and D.B. McNeil
The History of the Southern Railway by M.R. Bonavia (Unwin Hyman)
The Lancashire and Yorkshire Railway by John Marshall (David & Charles)
'The Magic of Old Ireland' by Tony Porter, *Railway Magazine*, Nov. 91
The Schools 4-4-0s by D.W. Winkworth (George, Allen & Unwin)
The South Eastern and Chatham Railway by O.S. Nock (Ian Allan)
The Southern King Arthur Family by O.S. Nock (David & Charles)
The Waterloo to Weymouth Line by M. Baker (PSL)
The Works (150 years of Inchicore) by Gregg Ryan (CIE)
Top Shed by P.N. Townend (Ian Allan)
Wainwright and his Locomotives by K. Marx (Ian Allan)

Index

Note: References to drawings, plans and photographs are in **BOLD**.